Power Tools
for
GARAGEBAND

Creating Music with Audio Recording, MIDI Sequencing, and Loops

BY FRANCIS PREVE

D1568428

Backbeat
Books

San Francisco

Published by Backbeat Books
600 Harrison Street, San Francisco, CA 94107
www.backbeatbooks.com
email: books@musicplayer.com

An imprint of CMP Information
Publishers of *Guitar Player*, *Bass Player*, *Keyboard*, and *EQ* magazines

CMP
United Business Media

Distributed to the book trade in the US and Canada by
Publishers Group West, 1700 Fourth Street, Berkeley, CA 94710

Distributed to the music trade in the US and Canada by
Hal Leonard Publishing, P.O. Box 13819, Milwaukee, WI 53213

Text and cover design by Doug Gordon
Composition by Maureen Forys, Happenstance Type-O-Rama

Library of Congress Catalog Control Number: 2004018667

ISBN: 0-87930-823-0

Printed in the United States of America

04 05 06 07 08   5 4 3 2 1

This book is dedicated to my fiancé and partner,
Seabrook Jones – without whom life and love
would be infinitely less interesting.

Contents

A Note from the Editor

Here are your choices: You can listen to an old guy reminisce about the way music technology used to be, or wade through some gee-whiz PR about how wonderful this book is — or would you prefer to tackle a brief but depressing rant about the point at which optimism turns delusional? Those are the options on today's pull-down menu.

Let's start with the PR, and see where that takes us. *Power Tools for GarageBand* is the fourth title in Backbeat Books' ongoing Power Tools series, for which I have the honor to be the series editor, and the second authored by Francis Preve. If you're looking to use your computer to produce professional-sounding tracks, you couldn't ask for a better wilderness guide than Francis. It's not just that he knows the technology inside-out and has a gift for explaining it in easy-to-understand terms; he also has a wealth of practical experience as a dance remix producer from which he can draw to provide concrete tips that will help you take your music further, faster.

Francis's previous Power Tools book, *Software for Loop Music*, provided in-depth coverage of several popular music programs, including Ableton Live and Apple Soundtrack. But as that book was nearing completion, Apple released GarageBand, which created a sort of mini-panic around the Backbeat offices. We didn't want to delay the loop music book, because we knew readers would be clamoring for it. So instead we persuaded Francis (it wasn't too hard, actually) to write a whole book about GarageBand.

We knew a couple of other books on GarageBand were in the works, and we wanted ours to be different. In keeping with the Power Tools theme, we decided to make *Power Tools for GarageBand* a book for advanced users — people who have already mastered the basics of GarageBand and now want to elevate their music to the next level. While GarageBand is undeniably easy to get started with, some of the things you can do with it are *not* obvious on the surface. Trust Francis to unearth and elucidate them.

Frankly, GarageBand is so powerful it scares me. (Note the clever transition to the second topic.) My first Macintosh, which I purchased in 1987 or thereabouts, was an SE/30. Except for the keyboard and the mouse, it was a one-piece machine, with one of those little black-and-white monitors and an awesomely capacious 20-megabyte internal hard drive. The only audio I ever got out of it came from a clever applet called the Talking Moose. (The Moose is still available for OS X, by the way, from www.zathras.de/moose.) At the time, my home recordings were created on an 8-track reel-to-reel tape deck. If I wanted to cut and splice portions of a recording, the only way to do it was with an actual razor blade, special tape, and a precision-tooled piece of aluminum called a splicing block.

Today, you can cut and splice audio with abandon using GarageBand. No razor blade is needed, just a mouse. GarageBand's sound quality is far superior to reel-to-reel tape, your fade-ins and fade-outs can be automated (I had to make the right moves with the faders on my mixer every time the song played), and the built-in effects processors are infinitely superior to the — *ahem* — spring reverb and 8-bit mono delay line I owned at the time. GarageBand's built-in software synthesizers may not be quite as flexible in terms of sound programming as my antediluvian Serge Modular synth, but they're a heck of a lot easier to use.

Time marches on, and technology marches right along with it. It's safe to say that if you're discovering the world of computer-based recording with GarageBand, you have a lot to look forward to. I certainly wouldn't want to over-hype the program, however. Francis uses the terms "professional-quality" sparingly in this book, and there's a reason for that. The software tools used today by professional musicians (myself included) are in many respects almost as far beyond GarageBand as GarageBand is beyond an 8-track reel-to-reel and a spring reverb.

But that's okay. You can get your feet wet with GarageBand and then decide if you want to jump into the deep end of the pool with a program like Digidesign ProTools, Steinberg Cubase, or Apple's own Emagic Logic Pro. Recording music in a computer can remain a weekend hobby or become a lifelong obsession. And a journey of a thousand miles starts with a single step.

What hasn't kept up with the technology (there's the segue into the third topic) are the opportunities for musicians to get their music heard. GarageBand tunes can be exported in iTunes format, blown into your iPod, emailed to your friends, and shared with other GarageBand users via websites like the ones mentioned near the end of this book. But getting too starry-eyed can be the prelude to serious disappointment. Establishing a career as a musician is just as hard today as it was in 1987, and probably harder than it was in 1957. You can do amazing things with GarageBand — but so can half a million other budding musicians. "Mix your hit," the Apple website says in a list of the things you can do with the program. But what does "hit" mean in this context? Not much. It's just a pumped-up way of saying, "You're pleased with your new song, and your mom says she likes it too."

MacPaint, the graphics application that shipped with the SE/30, didn't turn me into a full-fledged graphic artist, and GarageBand by itself won't turn you into a record engineer or producer. What it *will* do, though, are several very worthwhile things:

You can easily create great-sounding, pulse-pounding music to underscore your digital home videos.

You can make, edit, and mix very respectable demo-quality recordings of your songs or your band.

You can discover a little about the world of professional computer-based recording — possibly enough to convince you your life won't be complete until you go further.

If you have no musical training whatever, and never thought you had any musical talent (or even if you did have a few years of lessons and gave up because your teacher told you you didn't have any talent), you may be pleasantly surprised to discover that musical inspiration and creativity are more easily come by than you ever suspected.

And you can have a boatload of fun along the way. The way I look at it, that ain't half bad. So fire up your Mac, pause for a moment of silent reflection and gratitude because you're not stuck with an SE/30 or a reel-to-reel, and then get jammin'.

—Jim Aikin

Chapter 1
What's Hot About GarageBand

Sea change. Paradigm shift. These terms shouldn't be tossed about lightly, because there's always something new and revolutionary happening in the music software business. But once in a while a product comes along that makes musicians really sit up and take notice.

In January 2004, Apple stunned the music production community with the release of GarageBand. How can a fifty-dollar (or free if you buy a new Mac) piece of software shock an entire industry? Well, prior to the release of iLife—the suite of software tools that contains GarageBand—if you wanted a production environment that integrated over a thousand ready-to-use loops, MIDI sequencing, audio recording, eight built-in synthesizers, three modeled recreations of vintage keyboards like organ and electric Clavinet, a bunch of sampled instruments (including a killer acoustic piano), and no fewer than fifteen professional-sounding effects processors, you could easily spend several hundred dollars and still not come close. Heck, the software instruments alone could set you back hundreds of dollars if you bought the boxed versions.

What's the catch? Well, for one thing, GarageBand is optimized for novice musicians with no previous experience using professional tools. Accordingly, there's no confusing mixer interface, since each track includes its own easy-to-understand volume and pan controls. Some of the deeper features pros use, such as automated control of synthesizer parameters (essentially, letting the program move the sliders using data you've recorded), are not supported at all.

GarageBand is also somewhat limited when it comes to simultaneous tracks. While professional recording software—combined with a powerful computer—can easily achieve track counts in the 64–128 range, GarageBand's practical limit is around 24 tracks or so, even on a souped-up G5 system.

Granted, software instruments and effects eat up more CPU processing power than their hardware counterparts—and let's be candid here, *Sgt. Pepper's Lonely Hearts Club Band* was recorded on a four-track tape deck. Of course, there *are* ways to improve GarageBand's performance. You'll need to delve deeper into these pages to discover those secrets.

Still, by and large, GarageBand provides all of the tools an aspiring composer or producer needs to create shockingly good-sounding recordings. In the right hands, the results can sound downright professional. It's that powerful.

Let's take a closer look at the types of tools that GarageBand includes.

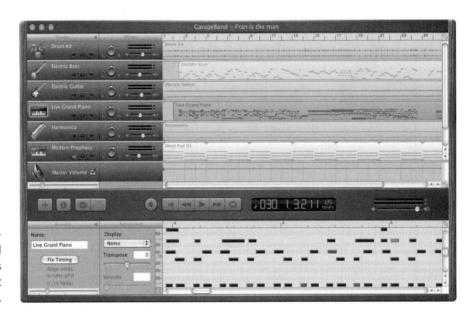

Figure 1-1
GarageBand's beautiful and uncluttered user interface belies the power lurking just below its surface.

Loops

The easiest way to make music with GarageBand is to rely on its collection of Apple Loops. What's an Apple Loop, you ask?

An Apple Loop is a segment of sound, such as a drum pattern or a guitar riff. When played by GarageBand, it will automatically be synchronized with the song's tempo and repeated—that is, looped—to create a groove. By combining various loops, then arranging them along GarageBand's timeline (so that they don't all play at once throughout the entire song, which would be boring) to create dynamic shifts in rhythm and melody, even non-musicians can get a taste of how today's music is produced.

While some musicians may scoff that working with loops doesn't require talent, it's hard to argue against the success of countless artists—from rap to rock—who have created memorable, even timeless, songs using loops. In fact, pretty much *everything* you hear on popular radio these days has a loop of some form in it—and if it doesn't, the dance remix does.

GarageBand simplifies the whole process of composing with loops via Apple's unique loop format, which allows loops to be categorized by instrument, key, genre, even mood. These category tags are often referred to as *metadata*, a computer term for information that describes other information. The bottom line is that this metadata allows GarageBand to do nifty tricks like summon only rock guitars and drums with a dark mood, or synthesizers and percussion with a cheerful, intense vibe, all within an easy-to-use browser tool.

From the browser, you can drag and drop these loops into GarageBand's timeline, apply custom effects like distortion and echo, then arrange them into your own personal masterpiece. For more info on using loops in your music, be sure to review the basic concepts in GarageBand's Help resource. These can be found in the section aptly titled "Working with Apple Loops."

MIDI Sequencing

If you're a pianist, keyboardist, or a fan of modern electronica and dance music, you'll definitely want to experiment with GarageBand's MIDI sequencing tools. While an in-depth assessment of MIDI and how it works is *far* beyond the scope of this book, there are some basic concepts that you should understand as you begin your explorations.

For one thing, recording a MIDI sequence is more akin to writing sheet music than capturing a sound on tape. This is because the recorded MIDI performance consists exclusively of a list of which notes were played, when they were played, how long they lasted, and what type of gestural nuances that performance contained. A MIDI recording does *not* contain actual audio (sound).

Have you ever seen a player piano in an old western movie? Think of a MIDI track as being like the roll of paper in the piano. The paper controlled which notes would be played, and how long each note would be held. The mechanism within the piano then read the roll and recreated the performance using the actual piano as its "tone generator."

That's essentially how MIDI sequencing works, only *you* create the musical performance (unless you're using a MIDI-based Apple Loop, discussed in the Loops chapter of this book). Once you've recorded this MIDI performance, you can then go back and correct flubbed notes, fix your timing, and even change the type of instrument that will play back the notes.

If you haven't already read the "Working with Software Instruments" section of the Apple Help guide, be sure to do so, in order to understand the MIDI-related concepts discussed in Chapter 4 of this book.

Software Instruments

The MIDI sequences you record are used to control the array of software instruments—known as "Generators" in Apple parlance—that are included with GarageBand. One of the major benefits of the book you're holding in your hands is its in-depth coverage of each and every software instrument that ships with GarageBand. GarageBand's Help file contains very little information on how to customize the sounds of your software instruments. How do you make your piano more muted? How can you make your synth parts more aggressive? If these questions pique your interest, be sure to check out Chapter 5, where you'll also find a fair amount of basic information on how synthesizers work and the fundamentals of designing your own sounds.

Of course, if you already understand the essential concepts behind programming synthesizer sounds, then you'll probably be more interested in that chapter's analysis of Apple's use of synthesis terminology and the macros that shape the sound of each generator.

Recording Audio

If traditional instrumentation is more up your alley, GarageBand has you covered. You can record mono or stereophonic audio tracks, edit them using the same type of cut-copy-paste tools that pros use to sculpt Top-10 singles, and process them further with effects and equalization.

Guitarists can generally get away with simply plugging directly into their Macs using a quarter-inch-female-to-eighth-inch-stereo-male adapter cable (provided the Mac has an audio input; iBooks don't). Those who plan to record vocals, or an acoustic instrument, will require a preamp and microphone at the very least—preferably a semi-pro preamp and audio interface combo, along with a mic.

Selecting these peripherals is largely a matter of personal taste, budget, and OS X compatibility, so it's best to consult a reputable musical equipment dealer for guidance. However, once you have the tools configured appropriately, Chapter 3 will assist you through the sometimes thorny process of setting the proper gain structure so that you can get the cleanest, most professional sound from your recordings.

From there, you can begin to explore more exotic techniques like comping a vocal and stutter editing, both of which are also covered in that chapter.

Effects and Mixing

Once you've got the desired combination of loops, sequences, and recorded instruments, the trick will be to get the balance right, using production tools like stereo panning, volume automation, and effects ranging from bitcrushing to reverb.

The effects chapter explains the ins and outs of GarageBand's audio processing tools, with explanations of every parameter and guidelines for getting the most from each effect.

Once you have a handle on how each effects processor works, you'll be ready to mix your masterpiece. The mixing chapter takes you on a step-by-step tour of how to set up a basic mix, with an added focus on how to approach common instruments like drums, bass, guitar, and vocals. The mixing chapter also contains a section on troubleshooting your mix, which can be very helpful if (as sometimes happens) the sound doesn't live up to your expectations.

Expandability

Amazingly at this price point, GarageBand is expandable in several ways. Apple Loops from third-party developers can be integrated into its collection. Software synthesizers and effects plug-ins can be added—as long as they're in Apple's Audio Unit format, which most plugs are, fortunately. Finally, GarageBand is also ReWire-compatible, making it an excellent complement to Propellerhead's Reason software sequencer and other music applications.

GarageBand's expansion possibilities also include a fair amount of affordable or even *free* offerings ranging from loop libraries to sophisticated synthesizers and drum machines. You'll find the specifics in that chapter *and* on this book's CD-ROM, which contains many of the free goodies described.

How to Use This Book

The purpose of this book is *not* to serve as an entry-level tutorial to GarageBand. For one thing, Apple has created a music production tool that is so intuitive and easy to understand that it's actually quite easy to get up and running, even if you have no prior experience with making music. That's the whole point of the application.

If the integrated Help files don't solve all of your problems, there are several excellent books on the basics of GarageBand that cover how to get up and running in glorious detail, notably *Apple Training Series: GarageBand* by Mary Plummer (Peachpit Press) and *GarageBand Ignite!* by Orren Merton (Muska & Lipman).

Instead of rehashing the basics, *Power Tools for GarageBand* is designed to help budding musicians and producers take their existing experience with GarageBand *to the next level*, using the same engineering and production techniques that seasoned professionals use. From conception to finished mix, *Power Tools for Garage-Band* covers the nitty-gritty on how to get the most from GarageBand, with each chapter dedicated to a different aspect of its extraordinarily comprehensive tool set.

Since many of GarageBand's functions are interdependent, it's recommended that you review *all* of the chapters, regardless of whether they appear to be relevant to your specific musical pursuits.

For example, if you work primarily with Apple Loops, you'll find a lot of relevant information in the MIDI and audio chapters as well as the loop chapter. Some of GarageBand's loops are in audio format, whereas others are in MIDI format (though the MIDI loops can be turned into audio loops, as described in Chapter 2). While Apple refers to audio loops as "Real Instrument Loops" and MIDI loops as "Software Instrument Loops," this distinction in nomenclature isn't entirely accurate. Having been around for over forty years, synthesizers are most certainly "real" instruments. If synths are real, then all software instruments are real instruments. Conversely, if synths aren't real, then many of GarageBand's "Real Instrument loops," which contain recordings of synthesizers, aren't real.

To avoid this issue, this book will use proper production parlance wherever possible—including referring to concepts, such as audio and MIDI loops, by the names used in the music industry.

The effects and software instruments chapters feature concise descriptions of what's actually going on under the hood of GarageBand. Quite a few readers will no doubt make the transition to professional-grade sequencing and recording applications like Emagic's Logic and MOTU's Digital Performer. In order to ease this transition, those chapters will clarify some of the terminology Apple uses to describe GarageBand's various parameters and macros. After all, when you graduate to the major leagues, you can't reasonably go into a recording studio and ask the synthesizer programmer to adjust the "richness" control, when what you really want to do is detune the oscillators and/or add chorusing to the sound. Hopefully, this book will help to demystify proper terminology and concepts, making GarageBand's essential tools easier to understand and work with as your production skills grow.

Armed with this knowledge, you'll probably find yourself wanting more—more loops, more synthesizers, more effects. That's where the Expansion chapter and included CD-ROM comes in. Many of the developers discussed in this book have generously allowed their products (or portions thereof) to be reproduced on this book's CD, so that you can experiment with everything from filtered delays to exotic waveshaping algorithms. Best of all, much of the included software and soundware is totally free—or at least in donationware or demo format—so you can experiment to your heart's content with a clear conscience.

By the time you reach the mixing chapter, you should have a much better understanding of how *all* of GarageBand's components—loops, MIDI tracks, recorded audio, effects, and synthesizers—interact, so that your approach to creating a professional-sounding mix doesn't rely on clicking through presets until you hear something that sort of works. Instead, you'll be able to tailor the performances and effects so that you can realize the music that's in your head.

And isn't that why you started tinkering with GarageBand in the first place?

Chapter 2
Apple Loops

After playing with GarageBand's sizable array of Apple Loops for a while, you may find yourself wanting more. But if you're not ready to pop the hundred bucks for one of Apple's Jam Pack collections, don't despair. There's still a *lot* you can do with the loops that ship with GarageBand.

Since this is a Power Tools book, we'll assume you understand the essentials of how to select and add loops to your arrangements. We'll focus instead on tips for editing and manipulating Apple Loops using the same techniques that professional sound engineers and remixers use. Of course, these tricks will work on *any* compatible Apple Loop, so whether you're sticking with the loops supplied with GarageBand or amassing a collection of third-party samples and loops, fire up your computer and get ready to experiment.

Loop Browser Tips

When GarageBand's loop browser is activated, an array of loop descriptors rises from the bottom of the main window. While this gives quick access to a decent array of loops, more inspiring possibilities are not far away. Hovering your cursor over the dividing bar (where the transport controls reside) changes the traditional cursor arrow to a hand. When the hand appears, click on this bar and drag upward. Presto! The rest of your loop options are now available.

The loop browser is optimized to offer loops that are within two semitones of your song's key, so even though you can transpose Apple Loops outside of this range, you may not be seeing all of your available options. After all, some audio loops sound pretty darn cool when pitch-shifted to the extreme.

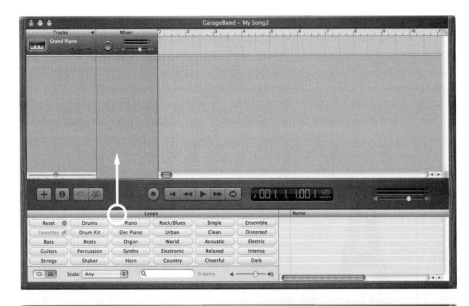

Figure 2-1
Grabbing and raising the divider that runs across the middle of the GarageBand window reveals *all* of the loop browser's categories.

To view *all* available loops, go into the preferences' General section and uncheck "Filter for more relevant results." This will allow the browser to display every loop in a selected category regardless of its original key, giving you considerably more options for your compositions.

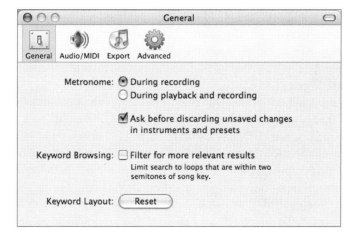

Figure 2-2
Unchecking "Filter for more relevant results" will allow you to peruse your entire loop library, as opposed to just the loops that are within two semitones of the song key.

If you've selected a time signature other than 4/4 time for your song, you may be dismayed to discover that all of the loop categories are grayed out. Hopefully Apple will fix this problem in a future version of GarageBand, but since most pop music is in 4/4, the problem will be invisible 98% of the time. You'll still be able to record your own MIDI and audio tracks, however, no matter what time signature you choose, and many of the loop editing tricks described below will work with your own recordings.

Green vs. Blue

In your GarageBand excursions, you may have noticed that Real Instrument audio loops are blue. You may also have discovered that the green MIDI loops can be transposed and edited, as well as reassigned to alternate software instruments. What you may not know is that these MIDI loops also contain *audio* data that allows them to be used as Real Instrument loops—in other words, as traditional audio loops.

To convert the loop format, simply *option-drag* a Software Instrument MIDI loop to the timeline, in an empty area below the existing tracks, thus creating a Real Instrument audio loop instead. (This command didn't work in GarageBand 1.0, but works in 1.1 and later versions.)

What's more, if you always want to work with Real Instrument loops for some reason, you can change the program's behavior so that ordinary dragging will perform the conversion. Choose GarageBand > Preferences, click the Advanced tab, then check the "Convert to Real Instrument" checkbox under "Adding Loops to the Timeline."

This trick is useful for a couple of reasons. First, software instruments and any associated effects use considerably more CPU power than audio tracks, so using the audio data instead of MIDI sequences is easier on your Mac's resources. Second, you can edit audio data in ways that yield different results than MIDI editing, such as creating stuttering or gated effects.

On the other hand, MIDI note and performance data can be edited directly, so if you want to change a few notes, tweak software instruments' parameters, and so on, you can customize green MIDI loops with relative ease. For tips on modifying these loops, please refer to the MIDI and Software Instruments chapters of this book.

It's also worth noting that some of the MIDI loops' audio data can sound slightly different from the real-time software instrument playback, due to the way that looping and time-stretching works. If you think there might be a difference, try dropping the MIDI file on a track adjacent to the audio track and do an A/B comparison. Chances are, any discrepancies will be minimal, but it's always worth hearing it for yourself and deciding which loop format to use for a given track.

Track Sharing

Another quick and easy way to make the most of your Mac's resources is *track sharing*. Any non-MIDI track can contain blue audio-based Apple Loops, the audio data derived from what was originally a MIDI-based Software Instrument loop, or even purple recorded audio—all on the same track. (GarageBand won't insert green MIDI loops on an audio track. If you drag a MIDI loop from the browser, it will be converted to an audio loop.) Using a single track to play several parts is simply a matter of selecting parts that don't overlap or play simultaneously, as each track can play only one sound at a time.

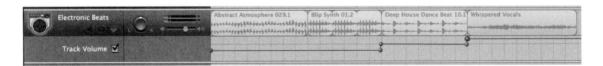

Figure 2-3
By having several loops share the same channel, you can make the most of your computer's resources. The secret lies in finding loops that benefit from identical processing.

The caveat with this approach is that you'll have to use the same effects and processing on all parts contained within the shared track. This means that if you have a groovalicious '70s electric piano track with phaser and echo applied, and you add a drum loop to the same track, the drum loop will have the same phaser and echo. For this reason, it's best to use this technique on tracks that contain minimal processing or EQ. A little compression or subtle reverb is okay in most situations, but whatever you add to one instrument in the track will be applied to *all* of the parts on the track.

If the levels of the parts in the track don't quite match—if one loop or audio recording "jumps out" during certain passages—you can address this with Garage-Band's handy volume automation tools. Just zoom in on the sections in question and raise or lower the level for each section accordingly. For more information on volume automation, please refer to Chapter 7, "Mixing."

Loop Cropping

Sometimes you don't need an entire loop, just a bar or two of its contents. This is often the case with drum loops that contain several variations over a two- or four-bar duration.

There are several ways to shorten or crop a loop within GarageBand. All of the methods work equally well, but some may be better suited to your preferred way of working than others.

For many musicians, the most obvious method may be to work in the track editor area at the bottom of the screen. By using the classic technique of highlighting the section(s) by clicking and dragging, then hitting delete as needed, you can quickly crop a loop to any desired size.

You can also crop loops directly from the timeline window. To delete the end portion of a loop, grab it from the *lower* right-hand corner and drag backward. To remove the beginning of a loop, grab from the lower left corner and drag forward. The resulting shortened loop can then be looped as usual by grabbing from the *upper* right corner and dragging to the right for the desired number of repetitions. Note that this technique also works in the track editor.

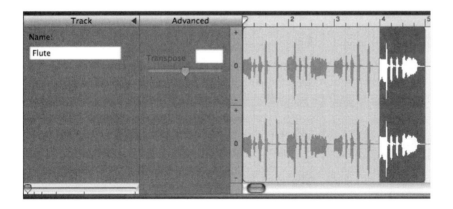

Figure 2-4
In the editor window, you can highlight any section of audio within a loop and hit delete to remove it.

Finally, you can use the split function (Command+T) within either the timeline window or the track editor to split your loop at the desired points. First move the playhead to the desired position, then split the loop, and finally select and delete the material you don't want. Once you've tried these approaches, it should become clear which one you prefer. Note that deleting matierial from the song won't affect the data stored in GarageBand's loop library. The original version will always be available if you need to get back to it, or if you want to use it in a different song.

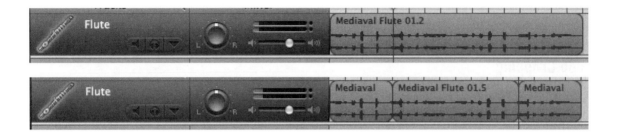

Figure 2-5

If you prefer to edit while in the arrange window, no problem. Just set the play head to the spot where you want to divide your loop into segments (top), then select the segments you don't want and use the delete key to remove them.

Beat Splicing

As you sift through GarageBand's collection of drum loops and club beats, you'll likely discover loops that you like *sections* of, but not the whole thing. This is where the beat-swapping technique can come in handy. Once you're comfortable cutting and cropping loops and understand the subtleties of channel sharing, you'll be ready to tackle this approach to making the most of your Apple Loop collection.

To get started, choose two loops that are complementary, yet different enough to be distinctive. This is largely a matter of taste, so use your ears and select loops that have similar character overall. Choosing disparate loops, like rock drums and a tiny analog drum machine, can sometimes lead to interesting results—but more often than not, such loops just sound awkward when combined.

To try this technique, select Club Dance Beat 003 and Club Dance Beat 009. Assign them to adjacent tracks. Now shorten both loops so that only the first measure (four beats) plays, then zoom into your arrangement so both loops' waveforms are clearly visible. (See Figure 2-6.)

Figure 2-6   Once this is set up, move the playhead to each quarter-note segment of each loop and use the split function to slice both loops into four equal beats. From there, select alternating segments in each loop—and delete them. (See Figures 2-7 and 2-8.)

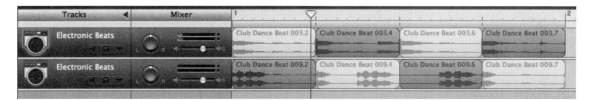

Figure 2-7

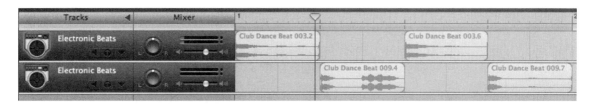

Figure 2-8

When you play your sequence, you should hear the two loops alternating beat by beat, creating an entirely new loop that contains elements from each. The secret to this technique lies in using a repeating rhythm when alternating between the loops. You can easily create splice patterns that are more complex than single-measure quarter-note alternations, but this is a good place to start until you get a feel for the tools.

Note that both loops still retain independent tracks and processing. By keeping the tracks separate you can add different effects to each set of loop segments. However, if your CPU horsepower comes at a premium, you may wish to have both sets of loop elements share a single track.

Fills and Rolls, Part 1

It's worth mentioning that many of the Apple Loops that ship with GarageBand include rhythmic variations every two or four bars. This makes it a straightforward process to loop part of each loop for your main groove, then switch to a variation every eight or sixteen bars as you transition to different sections of your song.

Even so, sometimes you can add more power and drama to your tracks by adding a snare or kick drum roll just before a transition, especially if you're working on a dance track or remix. Using a combination of loop editing techniques and volume automation, you can create fills and rolls ranging from subtle to intense, depending on your objectives.

Here's a quick and easy way to familiarize yourself with this editing approach.

Begin by selecting an uncomplicated loop like Club Dance Beat 007. Since it's a four-bar loop with a clap variation at the end, drag it out to eight bars so it plays twice. (See Figure 2-9.)

Figure 2-9 Now let's put an eighth-note kick drum fill on the final measure. Since we're focusing on that measure, set your loop points to cover the final measure only. Once you've done this, zoom into that measure and use the split command to isolate the first eighth-note segment, which contains the kick drum. (See Figure 2-10.)

Figure 2-10 Select the segment that covers the rest of that measure and delete it, so that all you have left is the original seven measures of drum loop followed by a single, isolated kick drum hit.

At this point, you're ready to create the kick drum fill. Select the single kick segment and copy it seven more times by dragging the upper right corner, so that it repeats for the rest of the measure. Follow this by option-drag-copying the original drum loop to a position after the fill so you can hear what the music sounds like when the loop reverts to the main groove.

Once you've completed these steps, show track volume automation and add three events, one at the beginning of the measure and two more at the end. From there, align the first and third automation points with beat one of the eighth measure and beat one of the ninth measure. Then drag the second automation event marker upward very slightly near the end of the measure, so that you create a moderate crescendo over the course of the measure followed by a rapid drop back to the original volume. For a bit of added drama, go back to the loop browser and search for a crash cymbal. Add the crash to beat one of the ninth measure (on a separate

Figure 2-11 track) and adjust its volume to taste. (See Figure 2-11.)

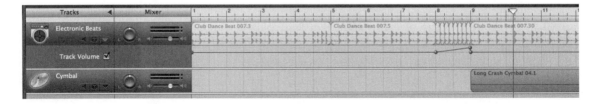

Fills and Rolls, Part 2

Another classic approach to fills requires two tracks. For this example, find another uncomplicated drum loop, such as Club Dance Beat 027, and create two adjacent tracks, both containing this loop. Since the loop has a one-bar breakdown on the fourth measure, shorten the loop to two measures for this exercise.

Leaving the first track untouched, select the second loop track and use the split tool on the last snare hit of the two-bar loop. Then delete all loop data before and after the snare hit. (See Figure 2-12.)

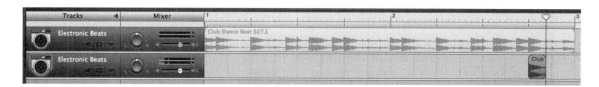

Figure 2-12

Now copy this single snare hit to several rhythmically interesting positions at the end of the second measure. It's important to *not* place any of these secondary snare hits in the same position as the snares in the original loop, unless you like obnoxiously loud doubled snares. Instead, add a few tasteful syncopated hits and lower the volume of the fill track slightly. When you play your sequence, you should hear a two-bar version of Club Dance Beat 027 with a nifty snare fill at the end. (See Figure 2-13.)

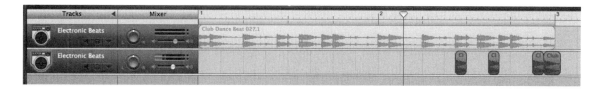

Figure 2-13

If you want to add some dimension to your drums, try adding an effect or two to the snare fill track. Flanger, phaser, echo, and reverb are all musically useful options, so try a few of these out and see if any of them works in context with your music. If you do this, the snare hits in the original loop won't be processed, so you may want to snip them out and replace them with identically placed hits on the fill track.

Slice, Dice, and Puree

Of course, there's a lot more to GarageBand's collection of Apple Loops than just drums. So let's use what we've learned so far to get some really wild effects.

From the browser, choose the country genre, and create a track with the Folk Mandolin 02 loop. Then, using your trusty editing skills, split the loop into 32 eighth-note segments. After that, create a new Real Instrument track with no effects. This will be used to temporarily hold the loop segments as you rearrange them.

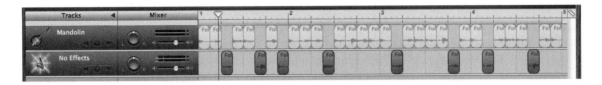

Figure 2-14
By slicing, then rearranging the segments of an audio-based Apple Loop, you can create subtle variations or wild electronica edits.

Now, randomly select a few segments and move them to the temporary track. Using both tracks to move the segments around, rearrange the pieces until you find a pattern that suits your musical objectives. Some combinations will sound fairly natural, much like the original loop but with the notes rearranged. Others will sound decidedly artificial, which can be good or bad depending on your tastes.

Speaking of artificial, you can get even more exotic effects by using this technique to combine two, three, or even more loops within a single track. One important consideration when using multiple loop sources to create patchwork riffs is that one- or two-bar assembled loops are better suited to this type of rhythmic quasi-random pattern generation. Longer patchwork loops tend to sound disorganized and haphazard unless you base your pattern on a repeating rhythmic or melodic motif, since the ear recognizes and locks onto shorter loops quickly—especially if they're matched with a danceable groove.

Rhythmic Gating

One of the most popular effects in dance music, hip-hop, and electronica is rhythmic gating—sometimes referred to as *transforming*. The term *gating* is derived from the classic technique of running a signal, usually a sustained sound effect, vocal, or melodic passage, through a *noise gate* and using a second rhythmic signal (such as a drum loop or percussion part) to open and close the gate. This results in the original signal turning on and off in time with the loop, thus imparting a chopped rhythm to the processed instrument.

Applying this technique to GarageBand loops can be tedious, but often the results are well worth it.

Begin by selecting an interesting, animated sustained synth part with a bit of harmonic and melodic movement. Contemplative Synth 01 is a great place to start. Since this loop is eight measures long, we'll shorten it to two measures so you can get the hang of this technique without incurring a wrist injury.

Figure 2-15
While it's definitely time-consuming, slicing a loop into thirty-second-note divisions is the first step toward creating classic rhythmic gate effects, also known as "transforming" in DJ circles.

Once you've shortened the loop, zoom into the first measure until it takes up the entire timeline window. At this resolution, the ruler should display eight ticks per quarter-note (thirty-second-notes). Use the split command to slice the loop at each tick, creating 32 slices per measure. Do this for both measures. (See? I told you this would be tedious. But don't give up yet!)

Now loop the first bar only and selectively delete slices until you create a rhythm that suits your track. This may take a few tries, but GarageBand's undo function will help greatly here. If you want to audition several different variations before committing, create additional "basic tracks" with no effects and option-drag (copy) *all* of your slices over to each of these new tracks before you begin. Then mute all but one of the tracks. This way you can tinker with each track until you find the perfect pattern for your song.

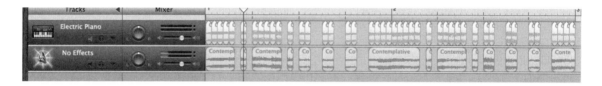

Once you have a suitable one-bar pattern, perform the same edits to the second bar also, perhaps with a subtle change or two for added flavor.

Note: Certain loop sounds may exhibit clicking when cut into thirty-second-note slices, even if the slices are adjacent to each other. If you hear this on one of your tracks, drag-select each set of contiguous slices and use the Join Selected (Command+J) function to glue the adjacent slices back together. This should eliminate most of the clicking. If you've got prominent drums happening also, the beats will mask any remaining clicks.

Rolling Your Own Loops

G ot some loops in Acidized wave or plain old AIFF format that you'd like to use in GarageBand? Well you can't use them directly, but you *can* surf over to http://developer.apple.com/sdk/#AppleLoops and download the free Apple Loops SDK (Software Developer's Kit), which includes full documentation on how to use the included Loop Utility. The process of creating loops is remarkably straightforward. Just open up any AIFF or WAV file in the utility and you can set a full range of attributes, including loop browser category information, loop length, even loop transient points—in a manner that's quite similar to using warp markers in Ableton Live or Sony's ACID. These markers enable GarageBand to intelligently time-stretch each segment of your loop in a more musical manner, thus delivering more realistic results, even with fairly extreme tempo shifts.

Figure 2-16
Once you've got your loop sliced up, you can experiment with different rhythms by deleting groups of segments. The top track shows the original slice edits. The bottom track shows the same edits after they've been rejoined using the "Join Selected" command.

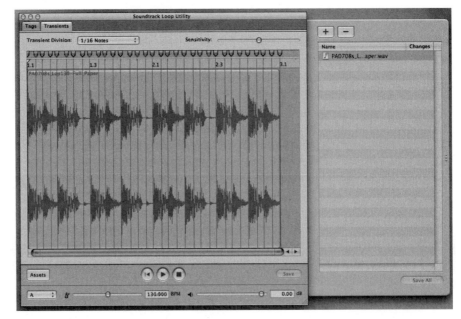

Figure 2-17
Apple's Loop Utility allows you to create your own loops from any WAV or AIFF soundfile—best of all, it's *free*.

Making the Most of the Loop Utility

Whenever possible, be sure to add key and scale information to your loop tags if you're working with melodic or chordal passages—along with the appropriate instrument type, genre, and mood descriptors. This is the only way GarageBand's browser will be able to organize the loops you create and add.

When working with rhythmic, percussion, or drum loops, pay close attention to the overall duration of each beat. If the groove is predominantly based on eighth-notes, set the transient division accordingly. If the groove is heavily syncopated, try using the sixteenth- or thirty-second-note settings.

Conversely, if you're working with flowing musical passages, try starting out with eighth-note or even quarter-note divisions. With certain material, these will sound better than smaller beat durations, which can sometimes impart a jittery quality to the loop when it's slowed down too much.

The sensitivity slider is a great way to really tweak your loops so that they perform well at a variety of tempos. As you move the slider to the right, more transients are detected and added. Unfortunately, no detection algorithm is foolproof, so you may find yourself with way more transient markers than you need. Fortunately, you can delete transients selectively. While the obvious way to delete a transient is to select it and hit the delete key, you can speed the process up greatly by simply grabbing the transient "handle" and dragging it upward, out of its lane.

Don't forget to audition your loops at a wide range of tempos before exporting them to Apple Loop format. At the bottom of the screen is a tempo slider for exactly this purpose. Here's a quick way to determine if your division markers are optimized: Set the tempo to about half of the original speed of your loop. This should make your loop sound weird and metallic, due to the manner in which the time-compression algorithm operates. At this point, begin tinkering with the transient division and sensitivity parameters. When the loop sounds as good as it can under these drastic circumstances, raise the tempo back to its original value. If you've listened carefully and made sensible decisions, your loop will be optimized for the widest variety of applications and is ready for export.

Note: If you're a fan of glitch or broken beats, setting your transients *incorrectly* can yield some wonderful digital errata at extreme tempo changes, perfect for freaking a laptop set.

Just because the loop utility does a terrific job of guessing the number of beats (quarter-notes) in a loop doesn't mean that's *your* intention. If you've got a two-measure (eight-beat) groove and you want it to be a metallic, stretched-out half-tempo loop, then input 16 as the number of beats and the loop will export accordingly. Of course, you can do the inverse as well, if you're after an unusual drum-and-bass or jungle effect. Just input 4 as the number of beats instead.

Chapter 3
Audio

While GarageBand makes recording live instruments and vocals a relatively painless process, knowing how digital audio works—and how to capture and edit a great performance—will help you to get the most from your mixes. Whether you're a hobbyist or a professional, navigating the ins and outs of the recording process is the first step to creating tracks that can survive the minefield between demo and final master.

In fact, since GarageBand records with 16-bit/44.1kHz fidelity, it's not unfathomable that a well-recorded demo track could make it all the way to an album or remix release. The secret lies in understanding essential concepts like gain structure, signal-to-noise ratio, and clipping. Once you've got a sound foundation in these concepts, you can further adapt your recordings with professional techniques like comping tracks and converting your audio to Apple Loop format for additional manipulation within GarageBand.

The first thing you need to know is that your Mac's built-in audio input is *line-level*. This means you can't plug an electric guitar or recording-quality microphone directly into it. Such signals first need to be boosted to the proper level. There are three ways to do this: You can use a dedicated device called a *preamp,* an outboard mixer that contains its own mic preamp(s), or a computer audio interface with built-in preamps. Without a preamp for your microphone, your signal will barely register on GarageBand's meters, much less be audible or have the proper gain structure.

If you have a Mac or Powerbook with audio inputs, you may be able to get by with a simple, no-frills, outboard preamp like M-Audio's AudioBuddy or a small mixing console with multiple integrated preamps like Mackie's 1202-VLZ Pro. Just connect the microphone or instrument to the unit, then adjust the preamp (and output, if applicable) according to the gain structure guidelines described in this chapter.

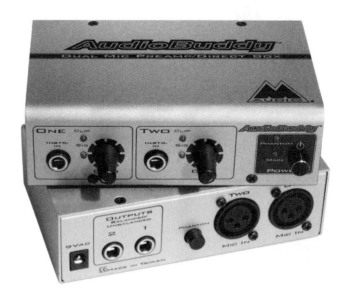

Figure 3-1
The M-Audio
AudioBuddy preamp.

Figure 3-2
The Mackie 1202-VLZ
Pro mixer.

If you're using an iBook—or want to have an all-in-one portable solution for your Mac or Powerbook—you may want to check out a USB or FireWire-based audio interface like M-Audio's MobilePre or FireWire 410. There are quite a few manufacturers that make excellent preamp/interface combos at different price points, so you may want to check out the offerings from Tascam, Digidesign, Echo Audio, Mark of the Unicorn, and others.

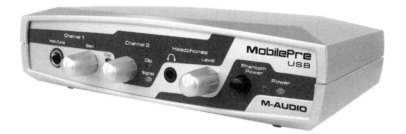

Figure 3-3
The M-Audio MobilePre
USB-based audio
interface.

Gain Structure

If you regularly record instruments or vocals and you want to get the most out of your recordings, you should familiarize yourself with the principles of gain structure. The term refers to optimizing the volumes or—in audio engineering parlance—the gain of your signals at various points in the signal path. Setting your preamp or input volumes incorrectly can diminish the quality of your recordings in several ways.

The three primary objectives for proper gain structure are maximizing your *signal-to-noise ratio*, avoiding *clipping,* and maximizing your available *digital resolution* (also known as *bit-depth*). Understanding each of these factors is the key to getting the best possible recordings from your equipment, regardless of its cost. Even a thousand-dollar microphone can sound awful if your levels are set incorrectly.

Signal-to-Noise Ratio

This term, which is sometimes abbreviated as *s/n ratio*, refers to the relationship between the low-level hiss and hum in your recordings (the noise) and the volume of the musical portion of the audio (the signal). Although digital recordings theoretically have a negligible noise floor, your choice of preamps, microphones, mixing console—heck, everything in the analog segment of your signal path—can introduce added hiss into your signal. On one or two tracks, you might be able to get away with a bit of noise, but when you add multiple tracks with a fair amount of hiss in each, you'll soon find yourself battling a wash of white noise.

The secret to avoiding this is to record your audio at the loudest possible volume short of distortion or clipping. At the same time, it's important to make sure that any preamps in your signal chain are not set too high, as they'll introduce their own distortion and/or noise artifacts to your audio.

Due to a phenomenon called *masking*—when two audio signals share overlapping frequency ranges, the louder signal masks the quieter one—a properly recorded track will conceal much of the noise floor inherent in the audio signal chain. Additionally, proper input levels will maximize the quality of your recording by taking advantage of

Figure 3-4
A properly recorded
sine wave (left) takes
advantage of the full
range of GarageBand's
16-bit resolution.
Setting all of your
levels too low can result
in a lower-resolution
recording (right), which
will sound grainy.

the full dynamic range of your system, giving your tracks a more up-front and clear sound.

One of the major benefits of good gain structure is making the most of your bit-depth. Since GarageBand records and plays back with 16-bit resolution, it's possible to create a true CD-quality recording with its tools. However, if your levels aren't loud enough, you won't be taking full advantage of your system's dynamic range. In other words, the noise floor will be too high. Another way to look at this is that if you're working in a 16-bit environment and your highest track levels peak at less than 50%, you'll be reducing the resolution to a lower bit-depth by not taking full advantage of the dynamic range that 16-bit offers. This can be perceived in the final mix as a grainy sound.

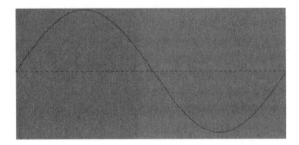 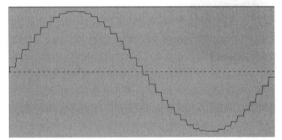

Clipping

Another recording pitfall is called *clipping*. Clipping is a flavor of distortion specific to digital audio. GarageBand records its audio with 16-bit resolution, which has a possible range of 65,536 values. Each of these values is assigned to a specific volume. So what happens if your signal exceeds this range and tries to go to 65,537 or more? Clipping.

Visually, when zoomed in, a clipped sample looks like a mountain range with all of the peaks chopped off and flattened. If the clipped segment is brief, it could sound like a click or a pop in the recording. If it goes on for more than a few milliseconds, it will sound like harsh, grinding distortion. For some types of industrial music, this can be useful. For everything else, it sounds decidedly awful.

In your efforts to improve your signal-to-noise ratio, you'll need to be vigilant about going overboard and introducing clipping. Clipping most often occurs at two places in the signal path: when the analog audio from your microphone or mixer is first entering the computer, and when the mixer in your recording software combines a bunch of signals before sending them to the output. If a newly recorded track clips, you'll need to turn down the level of the signal entering the computer. (Turning it down after it's in the computer won't work, because by that time the clipping is already part of the signal.) If you hear clipping on playback but you can't find it by inspecting the waveforms of your individual tracks, you're probably overloading the mixer by sending it too many loud signals at once. The fix is to lower the volumes of all of your tracks in a proportional way, so that the balance of instruments in the mix isn't disturbed.

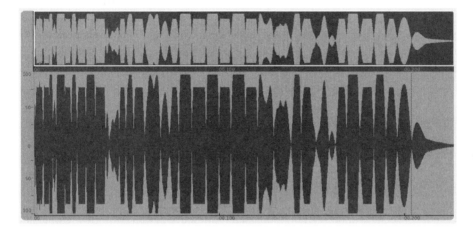

Figure 3-5
Clipped waves exhibit nasty digital distortion artifacts, which are caused by setting your recording levels too high. The flat-topped portions of this wave have clipped.

Making the Most of Your Signal

A good rule of thumb for establishing a healthy gain structure is to use the "75% rule" when setting up your preamps and signal levels. When working with a microphone or electric instrument with a pickup, begin by setting your preamps to approximately 50% of their maximum value. If you're using an electrical instrument (guitar, electric piano, etc.), turn its output volume up all the way. Then, while singing or playing your instrument, slowly increase the output volume of the preamp until you reach about 75%. The sound should be loud, but not distorted. Unless your preamps are really powerful—or your microphone is incredibly sensitive—you'll probably find that the signal is optimized when the output is between 50% and 75%. Now check GarageBand's meters. They should be bouncing around in the green and yellow range without going into the red. If the signal is too loud, back off a bit on the preamps until it is. Generally speaking, preamp output settings above 75% can sometimes introduce noise from the instrument or cause clipping at the recorder. By following this approach, you should be able to straddle the line between hiss and clipping without too much trouble.

A word of caution: When first setting levels, keep your monitors and computer input set at a moderate level. If your signal level is too strong due to incorrectly set preamp or output levels, you could blow your speakers and/or your soundcard. That would be very bad, and probably expensive too.

Editing Tips

Track Bouncing

No matter how fast your system is, if you're working with too many audio tracks and/or software instruments, you'll find yourself maxing out your computer's resources in your quest to create your masterpiece. Recording doubled vocals, layered harmonies, and/or multitracked percussion are all sure-fire ways to eat away at your disk and CPU usage.

How can you tell if you're overtaxing your CPU? Since GarageBand is designed to put audio processing first (and rightly so!), sluggishness in the user interface is the first sign of too much strain on your system resources. If you notice that your cursor is getting jerky, or if clicking on various GarageBand buttons results in a delayed response, then you're probably pushing your CPU too hard. Sometimes shutting down unneeded applications you may have running in the background, such as a web browser or mail application, will help, so try that first.

If, after closing all unnecessary programs, you still find yourself in this predicament, you can quickly regain valuable system headroom using a technique called *bouncing*. Bouncing allows you to create a submix of a group of tracks, such as backing vocals or instrument sections, which you can then reimport into your sequence. After reimporting the submixed tracks, you can then mute or even discard the original tracks, thus freeing up your Mac's resources. (Don't discard recordings until you're sure you won't need them anymore.)

First, create a copy of your original song file, so as to archive your source tracks in case you need to go back and rework the original material. Now, working from the copied file, decide which tracks you want to merge via bouncing. Mute all tracks except for those that you're mixing and adjust the volumes and panning of these tracks so that you have a good blend, keeping in mind that any effects that are active will be permanently added to the bounced mix.

Once you've got your mix set up to your satisfaction, export your song, then use the techniques described in the time-stretching section (below) to extract the exported files from iTunes. Place these files in your song's folder along with the original GarageBand sequence files, so that everything's organized.

Now, create *another* copy of your song, giving it a new name, then drop the bounced submix into this song and continue arranging and mixing. You can repeat the bouncing process with other instruments as well, but again, it's important to keep your original source files available in case you decide later that you need to make further adjustments to your bounced tracks.

Cutting and Pasting Sections

While there are myriad methods of recording and editing audio, there are a few tried-and-true techniques for optimizing your arrangements and making the best use of the material you've recorded.

If you're not a professional singer or instrumentalist, getting the perfect take can be an arduous task. After spending hours trying to nail a difficult chorus or background vocal, you may find yourself exhausted—or just plain out of inspiration.

Fortunately, GarageBand has you covered here. Using the editing tools, you can easily copy and paste the first chorus of your song to the second and third sections. This will leave you more energy to focus on getting great takes on the verses too. Make no mistake, this is *exactly* how hundreds, if not thousands, of chart-topping singles have been created, so there's really no shame in taking advantage of the same tricks—especially since GarageBand makes it so easy.

If you want to keep the integrity of your lead vocals by singing each chorus separately, you can still use this cutting-and-pasting technique effectively on the background vocals since they're blended into the mix anyway. Ultimately, this is a creative decision, but it's nice to know the technique is available as an option.

Comping a Performance

Another common recording technique that pros use all the time is called *comping*, which takes elements from several different takes, mixing and matching them to create a seamless whole that's better than any individual performance.

Next time you're recording a live track, try recording it three or four times, with each take on a different track. Once the performances have been captured, listen to each one critically. Perhaps the verse on the first track has the most emotion and energy, while the third track is more in tune. By cutting and pasting elements—sometimes even single words—from each of these parts, you can *comp* them together to create a track that contains the best of each take. Create a new, empty audio track—a Real Instrument "Basic" track, to use Apple's terminology—and then drag-copy the good bits from the separate takes onto this composite track, being careful not to move them forward or backward in time.

When using this technique, it's wise to limit yourself to no more than a few takes, since the process of sifting through and comparing each recording can be laborious. If you've got more than four takes, you may find yourself splitting hairs instead of focusing on the song itself. Sometimes a bit of imperfection adds musical character to a performance rather than sounding wrong. If you find yourself having trouble deciding which take(s) to use, give yourself a break and come back to it later with fresh ears. You may be surprised by the quality of your finished recordings if you take your time, letting them cool for a day or so before returning to work.

Stutter Edits

A classic trick that works well with recorded performances as well as loops is sometimes referred to as *stutter editing*. In plain English, a stutter edit contains a single segment of audio repeated a number of times, giving a performance a decidedly digital flavor.

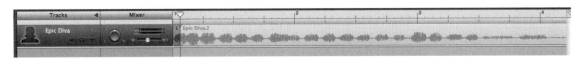

Figure 3-6
To create a stutter edit, begin by slicing the first sixteenth-note segment of a vocal performance.

Begin by taking a recorded part—vocals usually work quite well—then slice the beginnings of certain words into sixteenth-note segments, leaving the rest of the word and phrase intact. Now, move the rest of the phrase forward by a half-measure (half-note) and copy the initial sixteenth-note vocal slice repeatedly so that it fills up the space preceding the rest of the vocal.

Figure 3-7
You can copy the segment in Figure 3-3 repeatedly at the beginning of the vocal to create a classic stutter edit. The secret lies in finding appropriate words and syllables to emphasize within a performance.

Of course, you don't have to limit yourself to the beginnings of phrases. Try repeating sections from the middle or end of phrases. Experiment with slices smaller or larger than sixteenth-notes. Brian Transeau (better known as BT) has developed a technique he calls *nano-correcting*, wherein 128th-note (or smaller) slices are used to create rapid-fire stutters that happen so quickly that the listener perceives them as pitches. The secret here lies in experimenting with the power of GarageBand's editing tools.

Digital Glossolalia

In the words of Dr. William T. Samarin, professor of anthropology and linguistics at the University of Toronto, "Glossolalia consists of strings of meaningless syllables made up of sounds taken from those familiar to the speaker and put together more or less haphazardly.... Glossolalia is language-like because the speaker unconsciously wants it to be language-like. Yet in spite of superficial similarities, glossolalia fundamentally is not language."

The term *glossolalia* is often used to describe the vocalizations of the "speaking in tongues" trance state experienced by charismatic evangelists. It is also used to refer to the sacred utterances of various Native American shaman/priests.

What the heck does this have to do with GarageBand, you ask?

Well, if you're a fan of modern house or trance music, you've probably already heard what digital glossolalia sounds like: Tiny fragments of words, rearranged to create vocals that sound a little like jazz scat singing in a foreign language.

Recreating this effect is a total breeze in GarageBand. Just take your vocal part and randomly slice it into segments of varying lengths. Some segments might be an eighth-note long, others might be a quarter-note or sixteenth-note. The secret lies in using chaos and randomness as tools for creating something that no one would intentionally sing. That's what makes this technique so cool for certain types of music—especially dance tracks.

Once you have a bunch of interesting slices to choose from, start rearranging them haphazardly. Again, chaos is your friend here, so experiment freely. Let your ears be your guide. With luck, you should quickly come up with a rhythmic passage that captures the emotion and character of the original vocal, but presents it in an entirely new context, since the lyrical content is obscured.

Of course, this technique may also work well in traditional music genres like country, folk, or classical, depending on how adventurous you are in your interpretations of these classic styles. Still, for dance music, it's a time-tested way to add exotic spice to a remix or original song.

Opening the Package

GarageBand saves *all* of the recorded audio files from your song in the ".band" file. But what if you want to take the vocals from your song and use them again in a remix, process them further in an audio editor, or transfer them to a different sequencer?

You *can* access and extract the audio source files for use in other applications, and fortunately the process is quite painless. Simply Control-click on the song file and a menu of options appears. Select "Show Package Contents." This opens the GarageBand file as if it were a folder, revealing the components of your song. Don't touch the file labeled "projectData," as this is your sequence and arrangement info. Instead, open the folder labeled "Media." This contains all of your song's audio tracks. You may have to audition each audio file in the QuickTime player until you find the take you're looking for, but at least it's accessible, right?

Time-Stretching and Adjusting Tempo

Sometimes you'll record your song, then decide that it would sound better a touch faster—or slower. While GarageBand can change the tempo of loops, it doesn't directly support time-stretching audio tracks. Nevertheless, there's a simple, if somewhat time-consuming, workaround: Apple's Loop Utility.

The Loop Utility, discussed in the Apple Loops chapter, can be used on longer

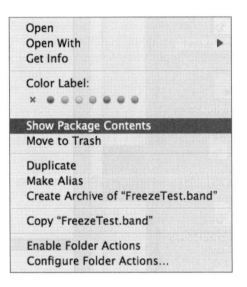

Figure 3-8
You can access the audio data lurking within your Garage-Band files by using the "Show Package Contents" command.

tracks also, but there are a few caveats that you'll need to be aware of. For example, while it's possible to record loops of any length, you'll find it easier to manage loop lengths that are exact measure multiples. That is, try to avoid creating loops with exotic lengths like 3.75 beats, at least if you're working in classic popular styles.

How do you accomplish this? Begin by setting your overall song and loop length so that its beginning and end are on bar lines, creating a segment that's a precise number of bars long—4, 8, 16, 32, or something similar. While it's not necessary to have the total number of measures be an exact multiple of four, doing so makes the loops slightly easier to manage for most common music forms. Besides, you can always crop the loops once they're in GarageBand.

Once your song length is set, solo *one* of the audio tracks you want to time-stretch, then export your song. This will create an AIFF file containing just that track—and any effects you've applied to it, so consider temporarily unchecking your effects if you don't need or want them in your loop, then export it to iTunes.

Now launch iTunes, select your instrument file, and press Command+R. This automagically opens the folder that contains the track you just exported. Drag the AIFF file to your desktop and give it a new name that's descriptive. I often include the song name, instrument type, and original BPM in the filename and keep all the files associated with a specific song or remix in a folder that also contains the GarageBand song file.

Once you've renamed and filed the song file, open it from within the Loop Utility. Then enter the time signature and number of beats. If you're unsure of the number of beats, take the number of measures and—assuming the song is in 4/4 time—multiply it by four. The result is your number of beats.

From there, apply the tips discussed in the Apple Loops chapter to optimize your loop for the updated tempo, then export it back to your song's directory, making sure to give it a new descriptive name so as not to overwrite the original file. This new file will be a stretchable Apple Loop that you can drop into the browser and incorporate into your song.

If there are other tracks that you need to stretch, simply repeat the above steps for each instrument you want to convert.

Chapter 4
MIDI

The MIDI protocol has been around for over twenty years now, and GarageBand's MIDI sequencing implementation is blissfully straightforward. With an impressive array of synthesizers and tone generators integrated in GarageBand as software instruments, the intricacies of hardware MIDI inputs/outputs, MIDI channel assignment, and exotic system-exclusive functions are largely irrelevant. Once you've configured your keyboard (or guitar or wind controller) interface via the Audio MIDI Setup tool, you're ready to roll.

Because of this simplicity—and the fact that many GarageBand users may opt to rely on the green MIDI-based Apple Loops—the tips and techniques in this chapter will tell you how to make the most of *any* MIDI track in GarageBand. Whether you're creating your own original loops and tracks using a keyboard as your input, or drag-and-dropping Apple Loops, these approaches should help you to make the most of the MIDI functions that GarageBand offers.

Reassigning and Modifying Instruments

As you work with the MIDI Apple Loops, you may find that you like the melody of a given part, but not the instrument itself. Since MIDI utilizes performance information and not recorded audio, it's extraordinarily easy to change which software instrument plays the part.

By clicking on the information button, then activating the Details view, you can select from a range of software instruments (or "Generators") that includes everything from electric pianos to analog-style synths, auditioning each option as the sequence plays. What's more, each of these instruments can be customized and edited to reflect your musical tastes. (For a full assessment of the capabilities of these remarkable synthesizers, please refer to the Software Instruments chapter.)

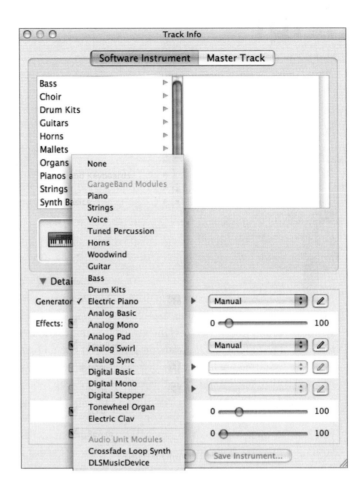

Figure 4-1
You can easily
audition alternate
software instruments
or edit synthesizer
parameters as a
sequence plays by
clicking on the
instrument selection
pull-down and making
a selection.

Reassigning Drum Kits

As with the instrument parts, GarageBand's MIDI-based drum loops can take on entirely new dimensions if you change the type of drum kit that plays the recorded rhythm. To get a feel for how dramatic this simple modification can be, create a track using the Funky Pop Drum 01 loop.

Now, open the information panel and select drum kits from the software instrument menu. This will display a list of all available drum kits on your system. While GarageBand comes with a nice selection of kits, if you've expanded your palette via Apple's JamPack or other third-party soundware (discussed in more depth in the Expanding GarageBand chapter) you'll have an even wider array of drums from which to choose.

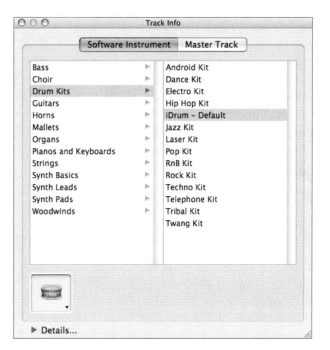

Figure 4-2
As with the synthesizer presets and instruments, you can also audition alternate drum kits as your loop plays—as long as it's a MIDI-based Apple Loop.

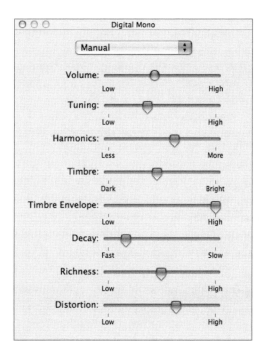

Figure 4-3
For even more exotic effects, you can even replace a drum pattern with a synth pattern by selecting a different software instrument. The Digital Mono instrument is great for percussive noise parts—the settings shown here are a terrific starting point for further experimentation.

If you want to get *really* obtuse, you can skip the drum kit options altogether and use software instruments instead. If you're an electronica fan, try starting with the Digital Mono generator and tinker with the tuning, timbre, timbre envelope, and decay parameters. From there, add a touch of echo for depth and added syncopation. The results, while a bit extreme, can sound great in both dance and industrial music. If you like the rhythm, you can drag single notes up or down as needed to create a part that's more melodic or plays a recognizable chord.

Editing Apple Loops

All of the data in MIDI Apple Loops is freely editable, so you can manipulate the note events to better match the key or melodies in your songs, incorporate new riffs into existing loops, or delete notes that don't fit your rhythmic or harmonic goals.

To demonstrate this feature, we'll use the 80s Dance Bass Synth 10 loop. (For some reason this loop is not categorized as a bass loop, but you can find it by typing "bass" in the browser's search window.) Begin by creating a new track with this selection, then double-click on it so that it appears in the editing window.

One of the nice things about the way GarageBand handles MIDI editing is that you can click on any note event and immediately hear it. You can also select groups of notes by dragging your cursor over the range you want to select. Drag-select *all* of the note events that are on the tonic (the key of the song) and move them up a whole-step. If your song is in C, you'll be moving the C's up so that they're D's. Notice how this immediately changes the character of the melody. (If you don't know a D from an E, don't worry: Just select some notes and drag them up or down. You can always use the undo command if you don't like what you hear.)

You can also draw new note events directly in the editor window by holding the command (Apple) key and clicking in the desired section. After entering each note, you can increase or decrease its velocity with the slider: By increasing the velocities of a few notes, you can add accents to a line. Another way to add notes is to copy any note event by selecting it, then holding down the option key while dragging the note.

Finally, you can simply play your keyboard controller—in record mode—while the loop cycles. No approach is "better" than the others, though some are more efficient for certain editing approaches. As with the other techniques described in this book, try them all and see which ones you prefer.

Adding Fills and Variations

Using the MIDI editing techniques described above, you can easily add drum fills and turnarounds to existing Apple Loops. For example, Southern Beat 01 is a straightforward, two-measure beat with a slight accent on the final snare hit. To create a simple, but classic, snare and kick fill at the end of the second measure, we shorten the final snare event by dragging backward from its end, so that the duration is one thirty-second note. Then we option-drag (and copy) this new snare event to the last two sixteenth-note positions and also drag another copy to the kick-drum event lane.

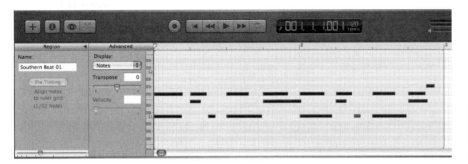

Figure 4-4
Here's the original MIDI information for Southern Beat 01.

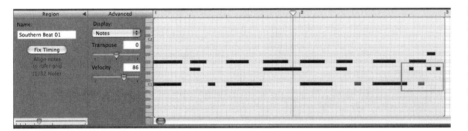

Figure 4-5
By adding a few grace notes (within the rectangle) for the snare and other drums, you can quickly add a custom fill at the end of Southern Beat 01.

From there, we can adjust the velocity of each note event so as to create a more human feel for this drum fill, or re-record the part manually from an external MIDI keyboard and then abstain from using Fix Timing. Of course, you can also create much more complex drum fills as needed, but in many mainstream genres, less is more, so pay close attention to your arrangement as a whole when creating fills, so as not to clutter your turnarounds too much.

Hocketing

According to the Virginia Tech Music Department's handy online dictionary (http://www.music.vt.edu/musicdictionary) of musical terms, hocketing is "a Medieval practice of composition in which two voices would move in such a manner that one would be still while the other moved and vice-versa. Sometimes this was achieved by taking a single melody and breaking it into short, one or two note phrases, and dividing the phrases between the two voices so that a quick back-and-forth movement of the melody would be heard."

As an aside, in 1325, Pope John XXII issued a bull banning the use of hocketing in music. Fortunately for us, the papacy no longer concerns itself with music theory, and we can freely use this technique in GarageBand without incurring the wrath of the Catholic Church. Best of all, hocketing is a piece of cake with MIDI sequencing tools, so let's take a look at how it's done.

Begin by creating two identical tracks using the 80s Dance Bass Synth 10 loop (which, like many of the other loops in this category, isn't particularly bass-like by *any* definition, but I digress). Keep the loop length at one bar and set your sequence's loop length to match.

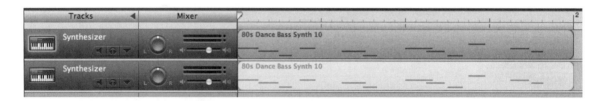

Figure 4-6

Prepare for hocketing a part by adding the same loop to two adjacent tracks.

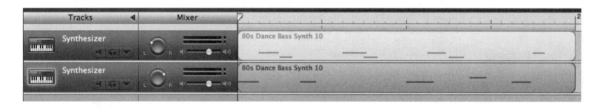

Figure 4-7

Then remove sections of notes from each of the loops so that one section plays while the other is silent, then alternates. From there, you can assign complementary or contrasting software instruments to play each of the parts.

Once you've done this, highlight, then delete all note events above C4 on the first track. Then delete all note events *below* C4 on the second track. (Note: I'm assuming your song is in the key of C. If you've chosen some other key, the MIDI part will be transposed up or down accordingly when the loop is imported.) When you play your sequence, the combined parts should sound identical to the original loop, since they're both playing the same Software Instrument, Analog Basic.

Here's where the hocketing fun begins. Select one of the newly edited tracks—either will work—and change the Software Instrument to something else, say Electric Piano. You'll now hear the same riff, but played by two alternating sounds. The difference can range from subtle to quite extreme, giving the parts a totally new sound.

For added character, try panning these tracks slightly left and right. This will give the performance more space and depth and will sound terrific on headphones. You may also want to adjust the relative volumes of the two tracks so that the two instruments balance.

Combining Drum Kits

By applying the above hocketing techniques to MIDI drum loops, we can combine elements from disparate drum kits, creating hybrid kits that better fit our musical styles.

Going back to our Southern Beat 01 loop, begin by creating two separate but adjacent tracks with this loop. Upon inspection, the kick drum is assigned to C1, the snare is on E1, the closed hi-hat is on F#1, and the pedaled hat is on G#1. Bonus points if you've already guessed that this assignment closely resembles the standard General MIDI setup—wisely, all of the kits in GarageBand adhere to this standard. Kudos to Apple for following it!

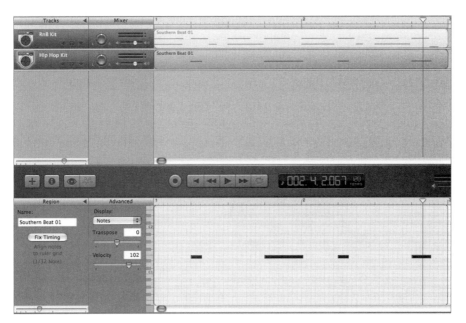

Figure 4-8
By creating two instances of Southern Beat 01 on separate tracks, then deleting various drum parts from each, we can substitute the snare from Hip Hop Kit for the original.

Since we now know which events activate certain drums, we can create a hybrid kit by assigning different kits to each track, then deleting selected drums as needed. For example, assign the first track to Pop Kit, then delete all of the E1 snare hits. From there, assign the second track to Hip Hop Kit and delete everything *except* the E1 snare hits. Voilà! A hybrid kit containing separate elements from each,

Best of all, you can now apply unique processing to the snare since it's isolated on its own track. If you want to make it more crunchy, add distortion. For a more spacious, ambient sound, try reverb. If you're really adventurous, you can use this technique to give each drum its own discrete track so that you can process, mix, and pan them individually.

Quantization Tricks

Like all good sequencers, GarageBand includes a quantization function, which is called Fix Timing. This feature maps each recorded MIDI note event to a timing grid that correlates to specific note values—sixteenth-notes, thirty-second notes, and so on—thus allowing users to record perfectly timed parts, free of human error. This is accomplished by selecting a loop or original MIDI sequence, setting the timing grid to the desired note value using the slider at the bottom of the MIDI editor, then clicking the Fix Timing button.

Of course, you may *want* a little humanity in your performances, with only certain sections "fixed." Fortunately, GarageBand has you covered there too. Just drag-select only the note events that require quantization, select the desired note value for quantization using the pop-up menu in the upper right corner of the MIDI editor window, and click Fix Timing. Working in this fashion allows you to keep the feel of your original MIDI performance, while correcting specific areas where the timing is off.

The included MIDI-based Apple Loops are either already quantized or feature performances with a funky, human feel—but that doesn't mean you can't apply the Fix Timing function to these loops. In fact, by changing the timing grid to a value other than sixteenth- or thirty-second-notes, you can often get an entirely new vibe from an Apple Loop.

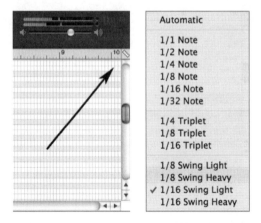

Figure 4-9
Clicking on the ruler icon (top) activates a drop-down menu with common quantization schemes (bottom), allowing easy auditioning of alternate timings.

By clicking on the easily overlooked ruler tool just to the lower right of the master volume control, you can directly access a menu of common quantization options. Selecting one of the 1/16 Swing options will shift the timing to a feel that's more appropriate for R&B, hip-hop, or house. The 1/8 Swing options impart a jazzy eighth-note-triplet feel. Switching a loop from straight sixteenth-notes to eighth-notes and adding a touch of rhythmic, dotted-eighth-note echo can give it a new lease on life, so when you're auditioning Apple Loops, keep in mind that with a few clicks of the Fix Timing tool—and an alternative Software Instrument setting—you can easily create an entirely new groove.

Mod Wheel Controller Tricks

The modulation wheel on most keyboard controllers sends MIDI information that changes the sound of various Software Instruments in musically interesting ways. If you've fooled around with this function, you may have assumed it only adds vibrato to a sound, as this is the most common configuration for GarageBand's soft-synths. Dig a little deeper, though, and you'll discover that several of the Software Instruments allow the mod wheel to adjust other musically useful parameters, further adding to the unique flavor of certain instruments.

For instance, on the Electric Piano instrument, moving the mod wheel upward adds a lovely—and idiomatically accurate—autopanning element to the sound, much like the original Fender Rhodes and Wurlitzer models that this instrument emulates.

On the Analog Pad synth, the mod wheel controls the setting of the filter cutoff, allowing you to add harmonic swells as you play. Trance and electronica fans take note, this is a terrific way to get those dramatic morphing effects that have become a staple of epic remixes.

The Digital Mono instrument features mod wheel control over a patch's timbre parameter, adding a bit of metallic hardness and brilliance to a sound as it's played. This is similar to opening the cutoff frequency, but with a more digital edge.

Finally, the Digital Stepper synth routes the mod wheel's control to an array of parameters that gives the sound of smoothly morphing through the settings of the harmonics parameter. For electronica, this is a terrific way to add dynamic character and animation to a loop or lead line.

As for other controllers, it's worth mentioning that on the Tonewheel Organ instrument, the damper pedal controls the brake function on the Leslie rotating speaker emulation, changing the speed of rotation when depressed.

Certain instruments rely on MIDI note velocity to change the character of their sound, allowing for interesting dynamic variations based on how hard you hit the keys. The acoustic guitars are perfect examples: When the velocity exceeds a value of 124, the sample switches to a gorgeous upward bent note, adding a lot of realism to the instrument.

You can edit or create smooth mod wheel and pitch-bend transitions directly within the MIDI track editor by selecting "modulation" or "pitchbend" from the display pull-down. For more information on how to do this, check out the GarageBand Help section titled "Editing controller information in a Software Instrument region."

Echo Tricks

Echo is a wonderful effect for adding syncopation and rhythmic complexity to a riff or chord progression. The secret lies in making room for the effect to breathe, otherwise you may simply succeed in creating a muddy mess. Used with restraint, echo can even be made to work well on a bass line. Two classic examples of bass echo include "For the Love of Money" by The O'Jays and "Rock On" by David Essex.

If you want to use echo in unique and exotic ways, add it to a new track *before* you start creating your original sequences. Set up a delay time that matches your song's rhythm, then start experimenting with minimalist parts that don't get in the way of the echo. If you prefer using MIDI loops, find one that generally fits your song, then delete notes as needed to clear out space for the echoed signal.

Either approach can work wonders for your tracks; it's just a matter of understanding the fine line between clever and clutter.

For more information on setting up GarageBand's echo parameter, please refer to the Effects chapter.

Chapter 5
Software Instruments

GarageBand's software instruments provide a surprising amount of flexibility for creating great-sounding synthesized and sample-based instrument parts. Each of the software instruments—known as "Generators" in Applespeak—uses a slightly different method for its tone generation. Becoming familiar with how audio synthesis works will help you make the most of these tools in your music productions.

While an in-depth analysis of how synthesizers work is far beyond the scope of this book, this chapter should serve as an overview and introduction to the world of software-based synthesizers and how to get the instruments in GarageBand to create the types of sounds you want for your music. If you want to dig deeper into the world of synthesis, I strongly urge you to pick up Jim Aikin's excellent—and thorough—tome on synthesizers, *Power Tools for Synthesizer Programming* (also available from Backbeat Books).

Synthesizer Basics

The most common method of synthesis—and the type that is available in the majority of GarageBand's software instruments—is called *subtractive synthesis*. What this means is that the synthesis algorithms under the hoods of these instruments work by *subtracting* (removing) certain parts of the sound from a harmonically rich audio signal. This signal comes from a device called an oscillator. It's worth noting that GarageBand generally eschews this type of terminology in favor of simpler words, which can be a trifle confusing if you're already familiar with traditional synthesis, or if you start with GarageBand and later move on to another music production environment.

Figure 5-1
The signal path and
signal processing in a
home stereo resemble
what happens in a
synthesizer.

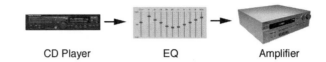

CD Player   EQ   Amplifier

One analogy for this type of synthesis-based sound generation is that of a home stereo. On a stereo, you have a CD player (the original sound source) whose output can be processed by equalizer controls (a set of audio filters) and then amplified and routed to a set of speakers.

Figure 5-2
In a classic subtrac-
tive synthesizer, the
oscillator(s) are
processed by a filter,
then sent to an ampli-
fication circuit—
or algorithm.

Oscillator   Filter   Amplifier

Subtractive synthesizers work in similar fashion. A sound source—known as an oscillator, or in some cases, an audio recording called a *sample*—is processed by a *filter*, which subtracts some of the frequency content from the sound source. After the filter stage, the sound is routed to an amplification module, which includes controls that govern how the sound's volume changes over the course of a single note. The volume-changing functions are commonly referred to as an *envelope*.

Each of GarageBand's software instruments offers a different set of editing functions for customizing its sound. Some of these software instruments are *sample-based*—that is, their sound source consists of a set of recordings of an acoustic or electric instrument that are assigned to MIDI notes so as to facilitate the playing of the recordings from a MIDI keyboard (or other controller). For example, the acoustic piano and string orchestra software instruments are based on sampling, as are several others discussed in this chapter.

Also included are several software instruments that are based on classic analog-style synthesis techniques. These rely on unchanging tones that are processed by filters and envelopes to shape the sound. Similarly, a few digital synthesizers are also available (though since we're working on a computer, *everything* is digital, so this is something of a misnomer). These digital synths use the same essential sound creation approach as the analog synths, but often include additional features for generating more complex waveforms from which to subtract frequencies using a filter.

Rounding out the array of MIDI instruments are a few vintage keyboard emulations, notably the electric pianos and tonewheel organ units. These are based on a type of synthesis known as *physical modeling*. Modeled instruments generate their sound by using mathematical or computer-based processes that serve to recreate the physical characteristics of the electro-mechanical instruments that the sounds are based upon. Fortunately, the available parameters for these instruments have straight-forward names, making it easier to understand how to edit the sound.

Since quite a few of the synthesizers in GarageBand share certain common functions, we'll discuss those up front so you have a better understanding of how they work.

Filtering

As previously mentioned, filters work by lowering the amplitude (volume) of specific frequencies from the signal produced by a synthesizer's sound generators. The most common type of filtering—and the type you'll find in the majority of GarageBand's synths—is called *lowpass* filtering. A lowpass filter works by attenuating the sound energy at frequencies *above* a set frequency, which is determined via a parameter called *cutoff* (shorthand for *cutoff frequency*). The frequencies below the cutoff are allowed to pass unaffected, hence the name of the filter.

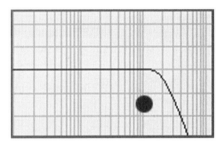

Figure 5-3
This graph, taken from Ableton Live, shows the attenuation slope and cutoff frequency of a lowpass filter.

Another common type of filter is called *highpass* filtering. This is essentially the opposite of lowpass filtering and works by attenuating frequency content *below* the cutoff frequency, thus thinning out the signal and making it thinner and more "trebly." The Analog Pad software instrument includes highpass filters in addition to its lowpass tools. While you won't see any slider labeled highpass, the character slider produces a highpass output when moved over toward the "sharp" side.

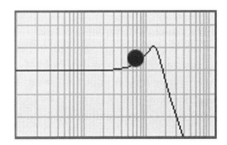

Figure 5-4
Another lowpass filter curve, this time with resonance boosted at the cutoff frequency.

Filters often have a parameter called *resonance*. Resonance creates a spike in amplitude at the cutoff frequency, resulting in a distinct pitch that tracks the frequency of the filter cutoff as the latter is manipulated. In practice, this imparts a squelchy electronic character that gives many software instruments their signature electronic sound.

Envelopes

Envelopes generally work by changing the *volume* of a sound as a key is pressed and held. There are also a few envelope options in certain instruments that change the value of the cutoff frequency in a similar dynamic fashion, adding harmonic animation to certain patches.

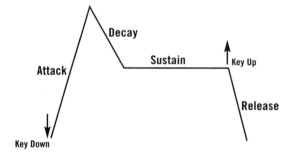

Figure 5-5
A standard ADSR
envelope, with key-up
and key-down events
indicated.

The four most common envelope parameters are: *attack time, decay time, sustain level,* and *release time.* The attack time parameter determines how the sound begins as a key is pressed. Short attack times give a sound an immediate, punchy character, whereas longer attack times cause the sound to fade in, like legato strings or a softly blown flute. The decay time parameter controls how quickly the sound falls from the attack peak to the sustain level. For example, an acoustic piano has a medium-to-long decay time if the key is held. Drum sounds, like snares and closed hi-hats, have fast decay times, giving them their percussive identity.

The sustain level parameter determines the overall loudness of a sound when the key is held. If this value is set to zero, the sound will fade to silence at the rate determined by the decay control. If it's set to any value higher than zero, the sound will sustain at that level once the decay segment has completed.

The release time controls how long it takes for the sound to fade out after the key is lifted. Some instruments, like bells, gongs, and certain cymbals, have very long release times, whereas sounds like Clavinet and xylophone have nearly immediate release times.

Not every GarageBand synth includes all four envelope segments. Some allow adjustment of the attack and release times, whereas others provide control only over the decay segment. Fortunately, quite a bit of thought went into deciding which envelope parameters are most relevant to the sound of a given software instrument. Chances are, you'll be able to modify most instruments to suit your needs—and if you can't find the synth control you're seeking, you can always use the effects processors to further tinker with your sounds.

What's more, several GarageBand synths, such as Digital Mono, Analog Sync, and Analog Pad, also provide limited envelope control over other parameters, delivering more dynamic complexity than volume envelopes alone. We'll discuss these in a bit.

Sample-Based Software Instruments

Several of GarageBand's instruments are based on Emagic's EXS24mkII software sampler, and make use of recordings of actual acoustic instruments. This gives them a convincingly realistic character that would be difficult to replicate using other synthesis methods. Of these sample-based instruments, some provide more adjustable parameters than others. Some include velocity-switching that triggers different recordings based on how hard you hit the keyboard. The acoustic and electric guitars are excellent examples of this dynamic functionality: As you hit the keys harder, different recordings (such as string bends) are triggered, delivering even more authenticity to your performance.

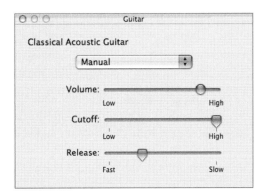

Figure 5-6
GarageBand's Classical Acoustic Guitar instrument includes control over volume, cutoff, and envelope release time.

The acoustic piano, drum kits, bass guitar, acoustic guitar, and electric guitar provide controls for volume, cutoff frequency, and release time. Adjusting the cutoff frequency allows you to give these instruments a mellower, more muted sound.

In practice, you can use this as an alternative to equalization or the treble reduction effects processors.

The release time slider is useful for adding a more realistic shape to the tones of the guitars and piano. While you can achieve the same effect by using a damper pedal (if your keyboard supports one), adding a bit of release time to certain instruments will give them a slightly looser feel, and long releases are great for slowly arpeggiated guitar passages—electric or acoustic.

Brian Eno fans should note that you can easily achieve a variation on his signature *Music for Airports* "underwater piano" sound by using the acoustic piano instrument, lowering the cutoff, and extending the release time greatly.

Another neat trick can be accomplished by lowering the cutoff of the various drum kits to about 25–30% and sequencing the various percussion and tom sounds to create a midrangey rhythmic rumble. This is great for adding support to minimalist-style compositions.

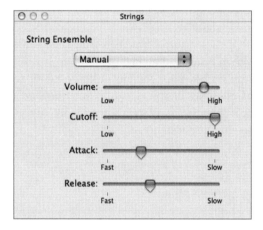

Figure 5-7
The String Ensemble also contains cutoff and release, but adds a slider for the envelope's attack segment.

The other sampled instruments—horns, strings, woodwinds, and saxophone—include the same parameters as the first group, but with the addition of an attack time slider that's quite useful for emulating horn swells and legato strings.

If you're a fan of soft pad sounds, try starting with a string patch, lower the cutoff frequency to tame the higher harmonics until the sound is rich and warm, then raise the attack and release times slightly to smooth the envelope contour. The result will give you a much more organic sound for chordal passages without sounding too synthy.

As for the woodwinds preset, try lengthening the attack somewhat, while reducing the cutoff to around 50–70%. This technique will evoke the old Mellotron flute sound that the Beatles used on "Strawberry Fields Forever." Adding a whisper of overdrive processing will enhance the effect further, but be careful to use restraint with the overdrive effect—otherwise the result will lose its vintage grit and warmth.

Analog-Style Synths

GarageBand's analog synths are based on Emagic's critically acclaimed ES2 soft-synth. Each analog instrument version includes a different subset of the original's parameters, optimized for specific sound-generating techniques.

Unlike the ES2 and other traditional analog synths, many of these analog synths eschew common parameter terminology in favor of terms that newcomers can more easily understand. While this makes sense for certain types of users, if you're already familiar with synthesizers you may find yourself scratching your head trying to understand exactly what each slider does. The confusion is further compounded by the fact that in some instances, a single slider will manipulate the values of several hidden parameters simultaneously. Wherever possible, I'll do my best to translate these functions into terms that more advanced users will recognize.

Analog Basic

The aptly named Analog Basic instrument contains a classic set of programming tools that are perfect for generating common synth textures. It can be used for bass, lead, percussive, and chorded parts, and sounds quite warm with a touch of chorusing, overdrive, and/or echo, which can easily be inserted in the Details pane of the Track Info window.

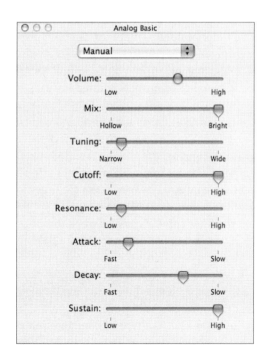

The adjustable parameters include volume, cutoff, resonance, attack time, decay time, sustain level, and two additional parameters that are unique to this specific synth: *mix* and *tuning*.

The mix parameter blends between the sounds of two oscillators. When moved fully left, the mix parameter gives a hollow sound that synthesists refer to as a *square wave*. Square waves are useful for everything from vintage video game sounds to ersatz woodwind and clarinet-type presets. The opposite end of the slider is labeled "bright." This is actually a *sawtooth wave*, which is useful for sizzling trance and techno leads, as well as emulating synth brass and string sounds. Of course, these examples merely scratch the surface of the type of sounds that can be created with this software instrument, as it's also terrific for the retro '70s and '80s textures that bands like Depeche Mode and Kraftwerk used on their early recordings.

The tuning parameter varies the amount of detuning between the two oscillators. When the slider is positioned at the "narrow" end, it functions as a fine-tune control for detuning and thickening the oscillator blend. As you move the slider to the right, this detuning increases significantly, which is useful for recreating those hard and bright lead sounds that dominate the trance genre. Beyond that, the tuning parameter functions as a coarse tuning function, bringing the oscillators into the two-note interval range, with steps for fifths, octaves, and two octaves at the maximum "wide" setting.

Analog Mono

Analog Mono is strictly monophonic—that is, it can only play one note at a time, much like a flute or trumpet—and features a parameter set that's rather similar to that of Analog Basic. Essential parameters include mix, cutoff, resonance, attack time, and decay time. Sustain level control is omitted since it's always preset at maximum, which makes the other envelope controls behave in an unusual manner. For example, the attack slider controls the attack time for *both* the loudness and the filter cutoff of this synthesizer. You can easily double-check this by setting the cutoff to about 30% and gradually moving the attack time upwards. The decay slider's behavior is a bit more obtuse, as it has minimal impact on the loudness envelope, since the sustain level is set to maximum. However, when the decay is full-on, it also adds a touch of release time to the sound. As with the attack control, the decay exhibits a pronounced effect on the filter cutoff dynamics when the cutoff frequency is set to anything below 80%, so it's probably better to think of this parameter as a filter decay control.

The mix slider also behaves differently in the Analog Mono unit than in the Analog Basic synth. In this case, the "hollow" (square-wave oscillator) side of the slider is also an octave *lower* than the "bright" (sawtooth-wave oscillator) side. While the behavior may be confusing at first, this type of configuration actually gives Analog Mono more flexibility for certain types of sounds, such as classic Minimoog-style bass recreations in which the oscillators are tuned an octave apart from each other.

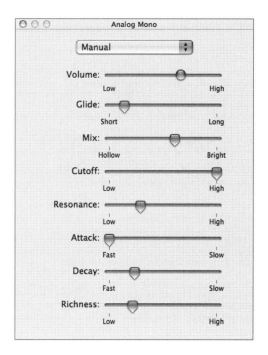

The *richness* slider detunes the oscillator sources in relationship to each other in a similar manner to Analog Basic's tuning parameter, but with the added twist of adding a tiny bit of randomness to the overall instrument tuning from note to note. This combination thickens the sound by giving it an organic, chorused texture.

Last but not least, there's a *glide* control at the top of the interface. Glide is also known in some circles as portamento, though frankly "glide" is a better term, as this parameter causes notes to slur in pitch from one to the next, much like notes played on a trombone or slide whistle. The key here is that in order to activate the glide effect, you need to play legato, allowing notes to overlap as you play. If you play staccato, the gliding is bypassed. Thus your playing style will dictate how much the notes slide around in pitch. A combination of longer glide times, high resonance, and medium cutoff and decay times will yield a sound that's evocative of the ever-popular Roland TB-303 BassLine. Playing your parts idiomatically is the secret, so it may take a little practice to achieve that sound.

If you're a fan of '70s-era progressive rock, you may be pleasantly surprised to discover that this software instrument does a terrific emulation of Keith Emerson's classic lead riff from Emerson, Lake and Palmer's "Lucky Man." The "New Luck" preset, found in Apple's JamPack, is ready ro rock.

Analog Pad

The Analog Pad instrument is optimized for lush string-like synthetic sounds not unlike those created by vintage keyboards such as the ARP Omni and Crumar

Orchestrator. As such, it features a slew of controls that don't directly conform to standard synth parameter names.

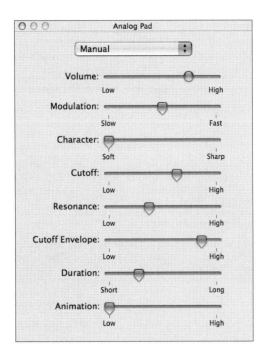

After the master volume slider, the next control is labeled *modulation*. This is actually fairly accurate, if you understand that the basic oscillator waveform that's used in this synth is called a pulse—or rectangle—wave. On traditional analog synths, you can often modulate the width of this pulse wave, which imparts a lush internal movement to the oscillator harmonics. Thus the modulation slider is actually a *pulse-width modulation* control. Moving it to the left lessens the speed and depth of the modulation, while moving it to the right increases both, giving the sound a rich, chorused quality. It also introduces additional detuning to this synth's oscillators—there are three in all—as well as adding a touch of the same tuning randomization that Analog Mono's richness parameter delivers.

Next up is the *character* slider. In broad terms, this adds an additional sawtooth waveform running through a resonant highpass filter (which removes low-frequency information from the sound, much like the bass reduction effect) to the sound of this synth. At the "soft" side, the highpass filter is bypassed, allowing all frequencies to pass to the standard lowpass filter. On the "sharp" side, a highpass filter macro kicks in, adjusting multiple parameters simultaneously and also adding some resonance to the sawtooth waves.

Cutoff and resonance controls function as expected, though there's some additional interaction with the character slider. Also, in the initial release of Garage-Band, the labels of the cutoff and duration sliders were reversed.

The duration parameter (mislabeled "cutoff" in GarageBand 1.0) affects all of the loudness and filter envelope parameters holistically, with "low" settings giving a strong percussive attack with a short release, and "high" settings lengthening these times for both the volume and the timbral content.

The cutoff control interacts with both the cutoff envelope and the character slider, the latter adding a highpass filter sweep to the sound so that it starts off thin and becomes more full as notes are held. With the cutoff set to "low" and the duration set between medium and long, you can add some lovely percussive synth attacks to your sounds.

Finally, the *animation* parameter is actually an embedded phaser/panner effect that moves the sound around the stereo field while simultaneously shifting its timbral content via a phase-shifting filter algorithm like those found in some classic "string machines."

Analog Swirl
Ironically, Analog Swirl doesn't "swirl" as much as Analog Pad. It has more in common with Analog Basic, but with tone generators that are based on Analog Pad's pulse-width modulation instead of Basic's hollow/bright (square/sawtooth) mix control.

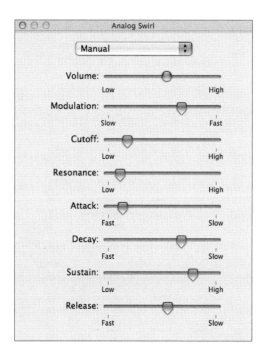

The modulated pulse waves are passed through a standard lowpass filter with cutoff and resonance controls, then modified by the envelopes, which include attack time, decay time, sustain level, and release time sliders.

There's another little wrinkle in the behavior of these envelopes. The attack parameter mostly affects the filter cutoff frequency, with just a touch of control over the loudness envelope. This gives Analog Swirl's sound a slightly percussive nature, regardless of the overall envelope settings. The other decay and release also affect both the filter cutoff and the volumes of the notes, but the sustain slider affects only the volume, not the filter.

Despite the obvious overlap between this and several other software instruments, Analog Swirl is terrific for riffing in a wide range of styles. The long filter attack sweeps are tailor-made for trance and progressive house, as well as a variety of dramatic film soundtrack–type sounds—and the pulse-width modulation gives this unit a slightly different flavor than its Analog Basic cousin.

Analog Sync
The last analog synth emulator, called Analog Sync, is optimized for a specific oscillator effect, referred to as *hard sync*. Without descending too far into the minutiae of this programming technique, suffice it to say that hard sync is used to synchronize the cycles of two or more oscillators, resulting in a metallic-sounding harmonic sweep that is simultaneously reminiscent of both the human voice and a flanged, distorted electric guitar. The adjustable parameters of this synth include sync, sync modulation, sync envelope, cutoff, attack, decay, and sustain.

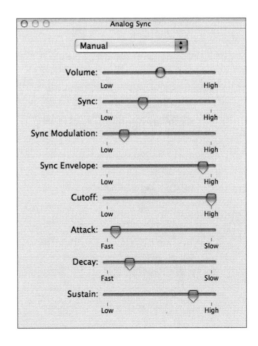

With all three sync parameters set to "low," the primary oscillator's waveform is a hollow square. As you move the sync parameter to the "high" range, the sync effect—created by changing the tuning of one of the synced oscillators in relationship to the primary oscillator—becomes progressively more pronounced. After a fashion, you can think of the sync control as a means for changing the basic harmonic content of your sound before it passes through the filter. Moving it to the right adds progressively more high-frequency content and harshness.

The *sync modulation* and *sync envelope* parameters allow you to animate the character of the oscillator sync, with modulation adding a cyclical motion to the animation and the envelope sweeping the sync value with each note event. Increasing the modulation parameter simultaneously increases the amount and speed of the motion, while the sync envelope parameter increases the intensity of the effect and is interdependent with the value of the decay parameter, with longer decays extending the duration of the sync sweep.

The cutoff slider functions as expected, rolling off the highs of the signal as its value is lowered.

The attack parameter contains another macro that controls the volume envelope, with longer attacks creating fade-ins. Interestingly, at medium-to-high settings, it also introduces a stereo flanger-type effect that causes the sync sweep to swirl around the stereo field—an exotic but welcome addition to this synth. In an interesting twist, the attack parameter's macro also affects the overall release time of the synth, with longer attacks also adding longer release times. While this isn't the most intuitive approach, it does allow a single slider to radically affect the overall timbre of the Analog Sync instrument.

As mentioned above, the decay slider affects the rate of the sync envelope modulation. It also affects the loudness decay, though not with the same intensity as sync. The sustain parameter also interacts with the sync envelope, with lower amounts creating more dramatic sweeps, since the decay parameter descends to the value set by the sustain level.

If you're a fan of either the Cars or the Crystal Method, you've probably discovered by now that Analog Sync is quite capable of recreating the signature lead synth sounds popularized by both groups.

Digital-Style Synths

While GarageBand's next group of generators is also based on the ES2 synthesizer architecture, they spotlight its wavetable and FM capabilities, while retaining some of the same synthesis elements discussed earlier. As with the analog emulations, each digital instrument is optimized for different musical applications, but all have that hard, crystalline character that's commonly associated with '80s-era digital synths.

Digital Basic

The digital basic synth includes a fair number of parameter names that are evocative of their effect on the sound, but not necessarily accurate in terms of what's actually happening under the hood—especially if you happen to have a background in synthesis.

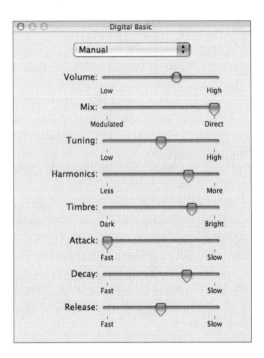

The seven sliders—mix, tuning, harmonics, timbre, attack, decay, and release—deliver a surprising amount of flexibility for their number, as Digital Basic is capable of creating textures ranging from ethereal bells to harsh industrial nastiness.

The *mix* control varies the overall signal between modulated and direct. The modulated signal adds new overtones, which are generated via FM (frequency modulation) synthesis. The character of this modulated sound is dependent on the *timbre* control.

The *timbre* control works in much the same manner as a filter envelope amount parameter, as it interacts directly with the attack and decay sliders. Moving the timbre slider toward the bright side increases the amount of filter envelope modulation, while the dark side decreases it, interactively adjusting the character of the overtones generated by the FM synthesis components of the synthesis engine.

The tuning parameter adjusts the pitch of the "direct" side of the instrument in semitone increments, similar to the transposition slider in the MIDI track editor. When the mix slider is moved toward "modulated," the tuning slider also affects the tuning relationship within the FM algorithm, which further modifies the harmonic spectrum of the sound.

The harmonics slider steps through a huge selection of digitally generated waveforms that have glassy, metallic, or bell-like characteristics. While the left and right sides are labeled "less" and "more," respectively, there's a multitude of harmonically complex waveforms to choose from in the middle region, so it's best to think of these labels as rough guidelines rather than as definitive descriptions. When the mix slider is all the way over at "direct," you can hear these waveforms clearly, as the FM portion of the synth is being bypassed.

The attack slider affects both the timbre (FM amount) and volume of the sound, as does the decay slider, while the release slider strictly controls the volume contour. Interestingly, raising the attack slider also seems to raise the sustain level, since instant attacks with instant decays and releases result in a plucked sound, while setting the attack to anything slower than immediate causes notes to sustain as long as they are held. Furthermore, the decay slider also controls the amount of FM in the modulated signal, so the added timbral harshness decays along with the volume in a musically interesting manner. The release slider affects only volume.

Programming idiosyncrasies aside, the configuration of parameters in the Digital Basic synth make it ideally suited to shimmery metallic sounds reminiscent of the classic PPG Wave 2.3 digital synth, which was a staple of '80s British pop and dance music. It's also fairly evocative of the bell-like textures that helped to popularize Yamaha's DX7 synth.

Digital Mono

Speaking of the DX7, Digital Mono features a set of parameters that allow even newcomers to experience a taste of the power inherent in FM synthesis, with little of the confusion and discomfort that this complicated technology sometimes causes.

The tuning and harmonics sliders work much as in Digital Basic, but with Digital Mono there's no "direct" output from the modulating oscillator in the FM algorithm that generates the sound of this synth. The timbre slider adjusts the overall amount of modulation applied to the carrier oscillator. As labeled, the higher the amount, the brighter the sound. The timbre envelope interacts with the decay slider, with short decays adding plucked and/or percussive transients. Longer decays lend a more organ or bell-like sound, and when combined with higher timbre and timbre envelope settings, deliver that classic overdriven hard FM sound.

The final two controls, *richness* and *distortion,* add oscillator detuning and distortion, respectively, which is handy, as it allows you to minimize the need for additional processing when adding a Digital Mono sound to your sequences.

It's almost too easy to get crunchy aggressive textures out of this instrument, so if that's your bag, this is a great synth to try. If you enjoy tinkering, try using low timbre and timbre envelope settings with a short—but not instant—decay. Depending on how the tuning and harmonics parameters are set, you can get percussive sounds reminiscent of kalimbas and marimbas, along with some interesting telephonic textures.

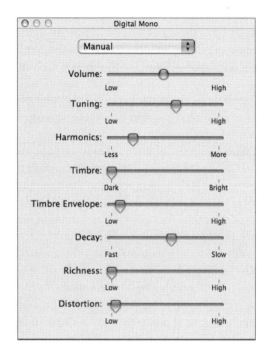

Digital Stepper

The Digital Stepper is a hybrid of analog-type and digital-type synthesis tools, as evidenced by its first synth parameter, *balance*, which adjusts the blend between bright analog sawtooth/pulse-type waves and the digital wavetable sounds found in the Digital Basic instrument.

The modulation parameter behaves rather similarly to the richness parameter found in the Analog Mono and Digital Mono synths, though it's not precisely a chorus in the strict sense. Instead, it adds a second, slightly detuned version of the oscillator source to itself. In practice, the result is darn close to chorusing, but the distinction is worth mentioning. Either way, it adds depth and animation to the instrument.

As mentioned, the harmonics slider sweeps through a set of digital waves that are nearly identical to those in the Digital Basic synth. In combination with the mix control, this slider makes the instrument capable of a truly wide array of sounds.

The harmonic steps control is where things get really interesting. What this parameter does is create a rhythmic, randomly stepped series of changes in the timbral content of a held note. If the steps are set to a small amount, the range of these steps is limited to waves that are close to the original wave, as set by the harmonics slider. When the steps are set to large amounts, the tempo-synchronized steps bounce around the entire range of waveforms available from the harmonics parameter.

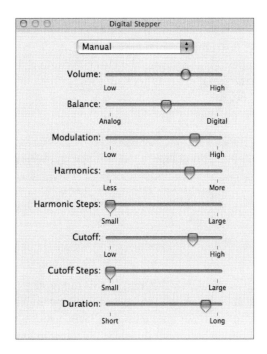

If you're a true synth geek, you may have guessed that this is actually a sample-and-hold LFO synced to your song's tempo (it plays sixteenth-notes, if you're keeping score), which is assigned to the waveform selection of the digital wavetable.

The cutoff slider functions as expected, adjusting the cutoff frequency of a slightly resonant lowpass filter. Of course, higher amounts give a brighter sound.

The cutoff steps control functions in much the same manner as the harmonic steps slider, only in this case the cutoff frequency is randomly changed in sixteenth-note increments. It's also worth noting that *both* the harmonic and cutoff steps controls add stereo panning effects in a stepped manner.

Finally, a duration control affects both the attack and release envelope segments, making this instrument quite useful for lush pad swells, along with its intended range of techno-trancey percolating rhythms.

Modeled Synths

While the above synthesizers cover an extraordinary amount of musical ground, GarageBand also includes three physically modeled instruments that are based on Emagic's award-winning EVB3, EVP88, and EVD6 plug-ins. They provide surprisingly accurate recreations of the Hammond B-3 drawbar organ, Hohner Clavinet, and Rhodes/Wurlitzer electric piano keyboards, respectively. Their inclusion in Garage-Band makes it wonderfully easy to invoke the classic sounds of mid-20th-century keyboards, for users who are more into soul, funk, and jazz than electronica.

Electric Clavinet

The Electric Clavinet instrument sports only one adjustable parameter (other than volume), called damper. This simulates the effect of muting the strings on a real Clavinet and affects the signal in a manner that is sonically similar to a combination of filter and volume decay.

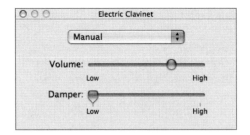

Even so, the behavior is slightly different in this instrument, since it's actually a model of a real Clav. If you want muted sounds, set the damper control to high. If you want more ring-off and that classic bright Clavinet sound that practically defined the Stevie Wonder recordings of the early '70s, set it to low.

Two GarageBand effects that sound terrific on a Clavinet are auto-wah and phaser. While several of the factory settings and loops take advantage of this type of processing, it's definitely worth tweaking the effects parameters to tailor the sound to your musical tastes.

Also worth mentioning is that the Electric Clavinet is quite useful for single-note muted guitar riffs, especially with a touch of rhythmic echo. When developing parts of this type, try writing the part with the echo active. You may find that you come up with unique syncopated riffs that you otherwise might not have, when playing your melodies interactively with the echo.

Electric Piano

Fans of soul, disco, and mellow jazz should definitely spend some time checking out the Electric Piano instrument, as Apple's version is one of the best-sounding models of these vintage instruments available anywhere. Really.

In the '60s and '70s, there were two main companies—Rhodes and Wurlitzer—that manufactured these electro-mechanical beauties. Each had its own sound, with the Rhodes sound being somewhat more popular with the jazz and soul crowd and the Wurli being favored by rock artists.

GarageBand's Electric Piano has modes for each model. The *tines* model is optimized for the classic, slightly bell-like Rhodes tone; the *reeds* model evokes the woody Wurlitzer sound. Of course, as with any instrument, your playing style is as big a factor as the timbre itself, but if you're looking for Three Dog Night and Supertramp electric piano textures, try the reeds model. On the other hand, if that laid-back Steely Dan vibe is your thing, go with the tines model.

Here, the decay slider works as expected, with no additional release characteristics added when set to maximum. However, extremely short settings will take you further away from a realistic emulation, veering more toward synth territory, which may or may not be to your liking.

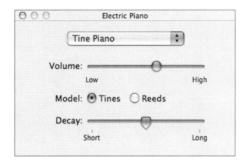

Downtempo and house artists take note: This electric piano sounds absolutely stunning on loungey, laid-back dance grooves. Try adding a bit of overdrive for a touch of retro grunge and a long, slow phaser for added authenticity. You may be amazed at how many classic keyboard parts were created with these two instruments alone. The secret lies in using effects processing rather than elaborate synthesis tools to get the sounds of yesteryear.

Tonewheel Organ

Last, but definitely not least, is GarageBand's outstanding Hammond B-3 emulation, called Tonewheel Organ. Its sound design parameters—drawbars, percussion level, percussion time, click, distortion, and rotary speaker modes—work synergistically to create an awesome range of organ sounds, from jazzy to hymnal to in-your-face rock and house timbres.

The original B-3 allowed individual adjustment of each of the first nine harmonics generated by its *tonewheels* via an array of discrete *drawbars*. In Apple's modeled version, the drawbars slider steps you through an array of preset drawbar settings based on popular sounds in a variety of styles. The "less" settings are useful for mellow jazz or textures more suitable for solemn church passages, whereas the "more" settings are bright and sassy.

Hammond organs also allowed you to emphasize the second or third harmonic with a bit of percussive punch at those frequencies. GarageBand allows you to do the same, via the percussion level and percussion time (decay) sliders.

Organ purists know that one of the secrets to an accurate B-3 emulation is a click at the beginning of each note. In the Hammond organ, this click was actually an artifact of the electro-mechanical action of their tonewheel design. In GarageBand, you can vary the amount of this added bit of attack noise using, of course, the click slider.

Traditionally, B-3 organs were amplified using another vintage technology—the Leslie speaker. A Leslie cabinet contained rotating speakers that whirled the sound of the organ about the room, creating wonderfully animated textures. As an added bonus, rock and jazz musicians discovered that these speakers could be pushed to the point of distortion, which added a gritty crunch to the sound.

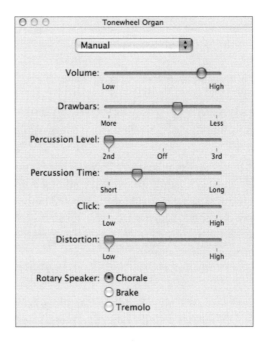

GarageBand adds this final bit of accuracy to the emulation in the form of distortion and rotary speaker parameters, which allow you to add that grunge via a slider and select among three rotary speaker emulations: chorale, brake, and tremolo. Here the sustain pedal has a special function: It allows the user to change from chorale to tremolo and back. Since this is a popular B-3 performance technique, its presence here demonstrates Apple's attention to detail and is a welcome addition.

Like the other two vintage models in GarageBand's arsenal of software instruments, the Tonewheel Organ can be used in a variety of contemporary genres as well as faithful replications of classic styles. In the early-to-mid 1990s, the B-3 made quite a comeback in house music, serving as the basis for countless tracks from artists like Crystal Waters, M-People, and Lisa Stansfield. The B-3 is also the source of many classic bass textures in dance music, notably the bassline from Nalin & Kane's "Beach Ball."

Chapter 6
Effects

As you work with your loops, software instruments, and recorded audio, you may find yourself wanting to add a certain something extra to each part—perhaps the ambience of a cathedral, or a shimmering animated halo that moves the sound around the stereo field. Thanks to GarageBand's selection of *effects processors*, it's a simple task to polish your tracks with tools much like those the pros use. All of the effects in GarageBand are based on the effects found in Emagic's pro-oriented recording and sequencing software, Logic Pro. While they have fewer adjustable parameters, the sound quality is identical.

The Details view for each track allows you to apply this array of effects to your musical parts, regardless of the track's origin—recorded audio, Apple Loops, or software instruments. Keep in mind that certain loops and software instruments come with various effects already active, so removing or changing these could radically affect the sound of these parts.

Every track includes a preset arrangement of effects processors, in a specific order that can't really be reconfigured for the most part, with the exception of the many effects choices for the two user-selectable inserts. Once the signal is processed by these effects, it can then be routed to the echo and/or reverb units for further modification. Later in this chapter, we'll discuss those tools in further detail.

The main purpose of these tools is to refine or enhance the character of a given musical part. Some instrument performances may contain too much dynamic variation in volume. Others may be too boomy, muddy, or shrill and require adjustment of specific frequency ranges to get them to fit into a mix in a more natural (or unnatural) manner.

The trick is in discovering ways to use these tools to give your songs their own sonic signature.

Since the initial two effects in the chain are fixed and can't be moved or re-arranged, we'll tackle them first.

Figure 6-1
This diagram shows
the processing path
for every Software
Instrument Channel in
GarageBand. After the
final selectable
processor, the signal
returns to the mixer
for level and pan
adjustment.

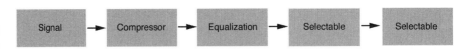

Compressor

This processing tool consists of a single slider that governs the overall intensity of the effect. What a compressor does—in simplest terms—is even out the peaks in volume of a given performance. For example, you may have a lead vocal that is more intimate during the verses and more aggressive during the choruses of your song. If the levels are set so that the louder chorus passages sit properly in the mix, you may find the vocals get lost during the verses. Optimizing the volume for the verses will have the opposite effect, with the choruses becoming too loud, perhaps to the point of distortion.

This is a perfect example of a track that requires compression. More experienced engineers and musicians may bemoan the fact that GarageBand's compressor doesn't allow access to the traditional selection of compression parameters like threshold, ratio, attack, and release. But that's okay, since the programmers at Apple have made all of these parameters interdependent and available under that one slider in a musically sensible manner.

Basically, as you move the slider to the right, you compress the dynamic range of your audio, making everything louder, including the quieter passages, while simultaneously taming the audio peaks. This makes it easier to set a consistent volume for a track throughout an entire mix.

Of course, not every track requires compression. In fact, too much compression can sap the energy of an enthusiastic vocal or riff. When working with the compressor tool, begin by applying a small amount and increase it only when necessary.

Conversely, compression can also be used as a special effect, giving tracks like guitar, bass, and drums a loud, in-your-face quality. This is often used in rock and dance music to increase the perceived impact of a performance. Try applying different amounts of compression to various types of musical tracks to get a better feel for what works for your style of music.

Equalizer

The second effect in each track's processing chain is equalization, often called EQ for short. Equalization is an essential production tool for changing the frequency characteristics of a given instrument. Chances are you've fiddled with EQ on your home or car stereo in an effort to make your favorite songs sound more powerful or give them more presence.

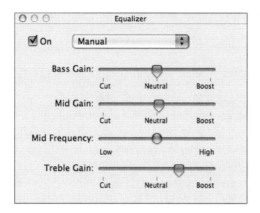

GarageBand's equalizer includes the two EQ parameters you're probably most familiar with: bass and treble. The bass slider adds or subtracts low-frequency content, while the treble function manipulates the high-frequency range, allowing a dull-sounding recording to cut through a mix more effectively.

In addition to these two parameters, GarageBand adds a third, adjustable range called Mid (midrange). Not surprisingly, this section governs a selectable range of frequencies between the lows and highs. The frequency slider selects the range to be processed, and the gain slider determines whether this range will be boosted or cut, and by how much.

Some important considerations when applying EQ:

- Not every track requires equalization. Wait until your mix is well under way before tweaking these parameters. Often, a track that sounds "wrong" on its own may sound perfectly placed once the other instruments in the mix are present. Accordingly, it's best to wait until your song has taken shape before deciding that the vocals are getting lost or the drums aren't punchy enough, and dialing in the EQ to remedy the defect.
- Less is more. Beginners often apply gratuitous amounts of EQ to tracks in the misguided hope that they can bludgeon the audio into submitting to their will. Wrong-o. It's best to think of EQ as a means to subtly sculpt your sounds with a nip here and a tuck there.
- 'Tis better to cut than boost. This may seem somewhat counterintuitive, but if you want to accent the high frequencies of a track, you may want to *subtract lows* instead of adding highs. Then increase the track level if necessary to compensate for the loss in sound energy. While this approach is more of a guideline than a hard-and-fast rule, it's useful for keeping your overall levels in order without

pushing your audio into the distortion range, since increasing the volume of a given frequency range will raise the total output of a track, which may have undesirable consequences. If you find your tracks fighting with one another in the mix, try this technique and see if it does the trick.

Other Effects

While the first two effects slots are hardwired to compression and EQ, the next two slots are fair game for an array of processors, giving you a degree of sonic flexibility. Before you go slapping effects on your tracks willy-nilly, it's important to understand that the order of the processors will greatly affect their sound. For example, placing a distortion effect before a phaser will impart a remarkably different texture than placing it *after* the phaser. (Try it and see for yourself.) This principle applies to pretty much every effect in GarageBand's bag of tricks. Generally, there is no "right" and "wrong" when assembling your effects chain, but it *is* important to carefully consider the effect you're after and apply processing accordingly.

Bass and Treble Reduction

The first two effects in GarageBand's processor menu are treble and bass reduction tools. If you have any experience with synthesizers, you may be able to figure out that these are actually lowpass and highpass filters, respectively.

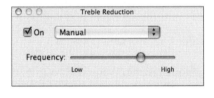

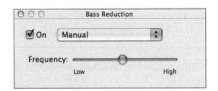

As discussed in the Software Instruments chapter, a lowpass filter works by attenuating frequencies above a specified frequency, thus dulling the sound of a given track. A highpass filter works in the opposite manner, attenuating frequencies *below* the specified frequency, making the track sound thinner.

Treble reduction is useful for taming a harsh instrument or drum part that's poking through a mix in an undesirable manner. Used sparingly, it's also quite useful for giving bass guitar parts a more realistic, blended sound in the context of a mix.

Bass reduction is a superb tool to use if you have one or more drum loops that are competing for the low end of your mix. Begin by choosing the loop that contains the kick drum part that drives your track, then reduce the bass of the other drum loops so that their kick drums are minimized, thus allowing them to remain fully present without muddying the low frequencies.

Another terrific use for bass reduction is in vocals or instrument parts that are too boomy. This can occur if the microphone is placed too close to the vocalist's mouth, emphasizing the low frequencies. This is known as the *proximity effect*. If you encounter this issue with one of your tracks, adjust the frequency slider to just under the point where the signal starts to thin out and then back off a tiny bit. This will get the offending part to sit better in the track without taking up too much of the bass frequency range, which should be reserved for the kick drum and bass parts.

Distortion and Overdrive

Distortion is a classic guitar effect that originated in the analog world. By feeding too much signal into a channel's preamp, then reducing its output volume so as to avoid toasting the speakers, you can get the amplification circuit to overload, adding new, harsh frequencies to the signal.

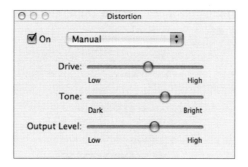

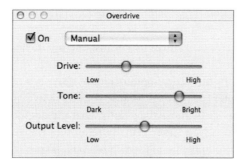

GarageBand's distortion effect includes three user-adjustable parameters: drive, tone, and output. The drive function governs the amount of distortion added to the signal. The tone control determines the frequency range of this distortion, much like an equalizer (which is essentially what it is). Often, adding large amounts of drive will increase the overall level of a signal, which is where the output control comes in: It allows you to reduce the volume of the distorted signal, keeping it in line with the rest of your mix.

Overdrive works in essentially the same manner and includes the same three parameters, but its sound is much more restrained and warm. Think of it this way: Distortion is best used when you want to completely shred an instrument, whereas overdrive adds organic warmth.

These effects are often overlooked when treating instruments other than guitar, and that's a big mistake. If you're a fan of industrial or experimental music, try applying distortion to a vocal track. It's perfect for that hard, megaphone sound. If dance music is your bag, try applying a touch—or a lot—of overdrive and/or distortion to a drum loop or bass part. It's a great way to add impact and crunch to percussive elements and will give bass or lead synth parts an aggressive, buzzy character.

Bitcrusher

Bitcrushing is an effect that rose to popularity in the mid-to-late 1990s and is based on an undesirable artifact of early samplers. Of course, when applied with intent, bitcrushing's distortion-like sound can lend a track a gritty, digital texture that's often associated with industrial music, French house, and electroclash.

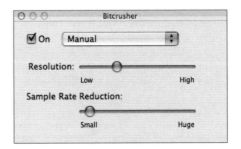

GarageBand's bitcrusher features two adjustable parameters, each with its own specific sound. The resolution slider reduces the bit depth of your recorded audio, transforming a clean 16-bit recording into a hissy, noisy 8-bit (or lower) recording. Reducing this parameter too much will cause your track to dissolve into a morass of trashy, distorted noise—which may be exactly what the doctor ordered.

The sample rate reduction slider actually resamples the audio in real time at a lower sampling rate, without the assistance of ADC filters, resulting in an aliased crunch that has become quite popular for house and electroclash tracks. Bitcrushing is an effect that works well on a variety of instrument types, including synths, guitars, and drums. Just for fun, try recording a vocal spoken in a robotic monotone style and apply liberal amounts of sample rate reduction. If you do it right, you should get a result that's quite similar to vintage electronic teaching toys from the early 1980s.

Automatic Filter

One of the more unusual effects in GarageBand's bag of tricks is the automatic filter. This tool allows you to create an undulating variation in the overall frequency content of a track. Some musicians have described the sound of this effect as similar to what one might hear if an instrument or loop were submerged underwater and then rose to the surface, becoming brighter and more present before descending back to the depths.

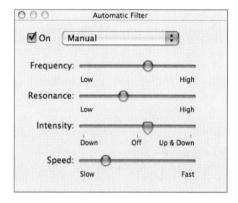

While this description may seem rather florid for a signal processor, it's actually quite evocative of the sound.

GarageBand's implementation of this effect provides enough versatility for a wide range of musical applications. The four adjustable parameters are frequency, resonance, intensity, and speed. The frequency function controls the base cutoff point of the filter, which is of the lowpass (treble reduction, as discussed above) variety. Resonance adds an emphasis to this cutoff frequency by increasing the amplitude of the signal very narrowly at the cutoff frequency. Increasing the resonance results in an added squelchy pitch that tracks the cutoff frequency as it changes. It's *extremely* important to note that increasing the resonance to maximum will cause the filter to oscillate loudly enough that it could ruin your speakers—or worse yet, damage your hearing (especially if you're using headphones). When working with the resonance parameter, use caution and make small adjustments until you get the hang of how this effect works.

The intensity parameter governs the amount and type of filter sweeps that this effect produces. Moving the slider to the right increases the intensity in an up-and-down manner, similar to a triangle wave or sine wave. At faster speeds, this is useful for wah-wah-type effects. At slower speeds, it can be used for morphing-style effects. Moving the intensity slider to the left changes the modulation type to a repeating decrescendo filter—a downward sawtooth wave, for synth aficionados. Again, the further you move the slider the more radical the effect.

Wisely, Apple has synchronized the speed control to the song tempo, so you can select from a wide array of modulation rates that correspond to bar lengths or note values. At the slowest setting, a full sweep executes over a 32-measure period (128 beats, if you prefer DJ-style increments). At the fastest setting, the modulation period goes beyond thirty-second-notes, useful for BT-esque nano-processing effects and bizarro synthetic textures.

It's worth noting that you can set the intensity to its center detent position, turning off the modulation entirely, which allows you to use the automatic filter in a similar manner to the treble reducer, but with the added bonus of being able to emphasize a specific frequency by increasing the resonance and tinkering with the frequency slider. This is a great way to tune rhythmic loops to the key of your track, creating a percussive pitched effect that can be brought in and out of a song at key moments.

Track Echo

While GarageBand includes a global echo effect that's available to all tracks in a mix (see the Master Effects section, below), you can also apply discrete echo processing to each track individually via the Track Echo processor, which includes the same four parameters as the global echo: time, repeat, color, and volume.

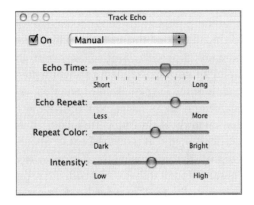

The time control is synchronized to your song tempo, so your echo effects match your music in a rhythmic manner. The shortest echo value is a sixteenth-note, whereas the longest time is a dotted half-note. The repeat parameter determines the number of echoes, and can extend well over eight measures, depending on your song's tempo.

The repeat color slider adds varying amounts of lowpass or highpass filtering to the echo repeats, with the center position adding minimal color to the effect. Moving the slider toward the dark value makes each repeat successively duller than the last. Moving it to the bright side makes the repeats become progressively thinner, with more high-frequency content. The volume slider controls the overall loudness of the effect.

Chorus

Chorusing is a classic effect that gives the illusion of multiple instruments playing the same passage in unison. By delaying the signal slightly, modulating its pitch slightly, and blending it back into the original signal, a chorus will thicken a single instrument nicely. GarageBand's chorus effect is blissfully straightforward, with two sliders: one for the intensity of the chorus and the other for the speed of the modulation.

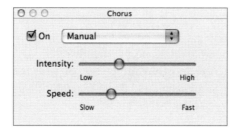

This effect is terrific for adding depth and animation to instrument parts of all types. For that sparkling '80s guitar sound, try adding some chorus to a slightly overdriven guitar part. Or if you want to turn GarageBand's gorgeous grand piano into a cornball honky-tonk upright straight out of an old Western flick, try setting the speed at around 25–30% and the intensity to the halfway point. While you're at it, get me a sarsaparilla, too.

Flanger

A close cousin of the chorusing effect is flanging. In straightforward terms, flanging sounds like a metallic, whooshing sweep that bears a passing resemblance to the Doppler effect caused by a passing jet airplane.

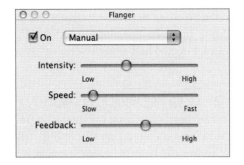

User-adjustable parameters on the flanger include intensity, speed, and feedback. The intensity and speed functions are identical to those in the chorus. The feedback parameter feeds some of the processed signal back into its input, thus reprocessing it in a signal loop. This generates an additional undulating pitch somewhat along the lines of the automatic filter's resonance parameter, but much more metallic-sounding.

Originally, flanging was a guitar effect, and it sounds terrific on gnarly, distorted power chords. Of course, flanging has tons of other uses in modern music production. Applying a flanger to bright percussion tracks like hi-hats or shakers will add motion, with the feedback control determining the overall metallicity of the effect. Flanging dense background vocal or choral parts delivers that classic Queen vocal treatment, whereas adding a touch to lead vocals—along with liberal amounts of compression—will impart an intimate, yet slightly electronic quality. You can add a mid- to high-speed flanger to piano and guitar parts for that vibrato-like wobble used in early tracks by Siouxsie and the Banshees and the Cure.

Phaser
Don't be fooled by the fact that the phaser effect has exactly the same parameters as the flanger. While they're both modulation effects, phasers rely on arrays of slightly offset filters, while flangers work by sweeping extremely short delay times.

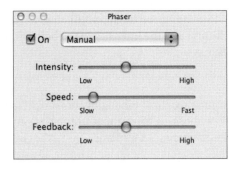

In plain English, the sound and texture of a phaser tends to be more smooth and less metallic than that of a flanger. Like a flanger, a phaser sounds great on guitars and percussion loops. Vocals get a much more psychedelic sound with phasing applied, making this effect a shoo-in for remixers and electronica artists.

Soul, lounge, and house fans take note: Adding a phaser and chorus to an electric piano or Clavinet is a great shortcut to getting that smoky, animated keyboard sound that defined classic tracks from Stevie Wonder, Steely Dan, and Isaac Hayes.

Tremolo

Guitarists know that tremolo is the secret to getting classic surf and country sounds. The way tremolo works is by modulating the *volume* of an audio signal, without affecting the pitch or timbral content of the instrument.

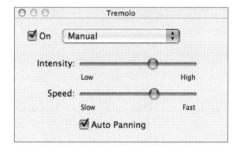

As with the other modulation effects, intensity and speed controls are provided (though unfortunately the speed can't be synchronized to tempo), as is a checkbox option called Auto Panning.

What's auto-panning? It's a stereo version of the tremolo effect that causes the signal to sweep back and forth between the left and right speakers. At slow rates with medium intensities, it's a wonderful way to highlight a musical part for headphone listeners. At faster rates, it can be somewhat distracting—and when applied to more than one or two instruments, it can really mess with a mix in a *bad* way, so use restraint when using this effect. A little goes a long way.

Side note to '60s and '70s pop buffs: The quivering vocal effect at the end of Tommy James's "Crimson and Clover" is a classic—and groundbreaking—example of tremolo applied to vocals.

Auto-Wah

Anyone who's familiar with classic '70s funk and disco should be familiar with the "bam-chicka-bow-wow" slinky guitar sound that dominated dance grooves, cop shows, and, uhh…racy films. The effect that generates this effect is called a wah-wah pedal, which allows guitarists to rhymically manipulate a specialized filter with an expression pedal. The further down you press the pedal, the more the filter opens up, and vice versa.

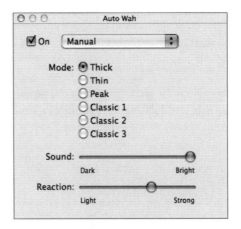

GarageBand's effects menu includes a variation on this processor, aptly called an Auto Wah. In lieu of a pedal control, the auto-wah effect opens and closes the filter based on the intensity (loudness) of the input signal. In the case of guitar, the harder you play, the more the filter opens up.

Adjustable parameters include an array of filter modes: thick, thin, peak, and classic 1–3. Each mode has its own characteristics; some are better suited to funky bits, whereas others are ideal for rock riffing *à la* Jimi Hendrix.

Other parameters include "sound," which sets the base level for the filter—that is, how this effect will sound with a moderately intense playing style. The "reaction" parameter controls the intensity of the wah effect.

You can get a feel for how the effect works by selecting a clean or rock guitar loop from the loop browser, then applying the auto-wah effect and tinkering with the controls, listening closely to how the modes interact with the sound and reaction parameters.

Once you get the hang of how this effect can be used, try applying it to drum loops and synth parts. It's also a great processor for Clavinet sounds, as that particular software instrument has a guitar-like sound to begin with and really lends itself to the wah filter.

Amp Simulation
One of GarageBand's most impressive tools is the Amp Simulation unit. While this effect tends to use more CPU horsepower than most of the other processors, it's

uncanny in its emulation of the sound of a real guitar amplifier, right down to the distortion inherent in an actual amp.

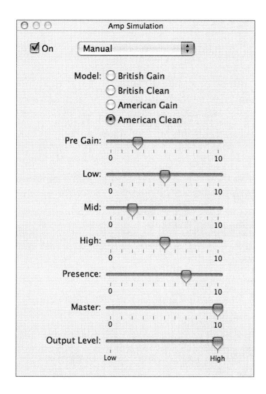

There are four models to choose from: British Gain, British Clean, American Gain, and American Clean. Each of these models is based on a real amplifier type, though the specifics aren't well documented in GarageBand's reference literature.

The pre gain slider affects the virtual input volume, with higher amounts adding increasing levels of distortion. This is followed by low, mid, and high controls for basic tone-shaping purposes. The presence parameter further emphasizes the high end, allowing the processed signal to really cut through a mix.

The final two parameters, master and output, appear to do the same thing: control volume. Why they're both included is a bit of a mystery.

As with distortion and overdrive effects, try applying the various amp simulation types to drum loops and keyboard parts. Even when you don't boost the pre gain amount to distortion levels, the simulation will imbue a more organic, raw quality to even the most electronic-sounding instruments. With careful adjustment you can also use the amp simulator for imparting a radio-announcer effect to a spoken vocal part. This is handy if you do film or commercial work and need to add some retro pizzazz to a voiceover.

Master Effects

The last two effects in the details view, echo and reverb, differ from the others in that these effects are *global*. That is, GarageBand has only one reverb and one echo processor, and you can send signals to them in varying amounts from any or all tracks in a mix, without having to create separate instances for each instrument. This is a sensible approach, as effects like reverb can eat up a lot of CPU processing power. Allowing a single reverb to do the work of many units gives you more room to add room ambience to your tracks, even if you're not on a top-of-the line G5 system.

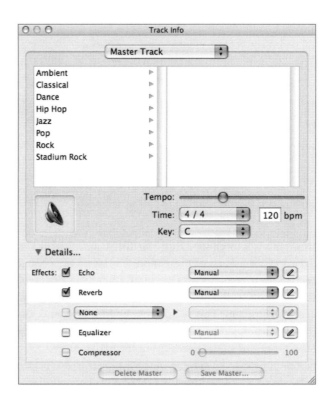

Figure 6-2
The Master Track's info window includes the global echo and reverb editors, as well as compression and EQ for mastering purposes.

Global effects like these are also called *send effects*. Essentially, each track in your mixer has two send busses—level controls that route some of the signal to auxiliary destinations, in this case the echo and reverb processors. When you adjust the levels of the echo and reverb sliders, you're really adjusting the amount of signal being sent to that effect. The output of the effect is then added to your final mix.

So how do you adjust the controls of these effects to tailor them to the sound you're after? Well, if you're not already intimate with GarageBand, you may be surprised to find them tucked away in the Master Track details window. You can reveal this track in your arrangement via the main menus. In the Track pull-down menu, select Show Master Track (or use the key combo Command+B). This will reveal the master track in your arrangement window. From there, select that track, show information, then reveal the details section. Presto! Your echo and reverb busses are ready for editing, along with a few other master effects that we'll discuss in a bit.

Echo

The global echo bus features the same set of parameters as the Track Echo processor discussed earlier in this chapter, so if you just want to add a touch of echo to a few tracks, this is the way to go—especially if you need to conserve CPU horsepower for other purposes.

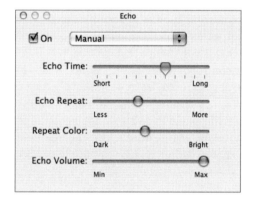

It's worth noting that the volume slider determines the *overall* loudness of all echoes provided by this effect. This is quite useful if you find your mix is getting too cluttered with echoes bouncing all over the place. Rather than adjusting the send amount for each track individually, you can simply lower the overall echo volume for your mix and quickly clean things up.

Reverb

The global reverb effect is used to create the illusion of acoustic spaces. If you want to make elements of your music sound as if they were played in a cathedral, a gymnasium, or a garage, this is the processor to use.

The reverb time parameter determines the perceived size of your simulated acoustic environment. If you want a giant stadium or canyon, use a long time setting. If you want a more intimate room or club sound, shorten the time. Note that longer times add a touch of delay to the onset of the reverb effect. While this simulates the true acoustic effect of a sonic impulse traveling to the physical boundaries of a space before reflecting back at the listener, it can also add an undesirable rhythmic effect to percussive parts. This is something to be aware of as you work.

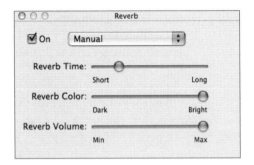

The reverb color control is used to change the frequency characteristics of the spatial emulation and works rather like the echo color control, with dark being more muted and bright adding more treble content.

Again, the volume control determines the overall reverb amount in your mix. As a rule of thumb, it's unwise to add reverb—especially long reverbs—to every instrument in your song. Try adding a touch to vocals or instruments that benefit from spatial ambience, like piano and drums. The application of reverb is a matter of personal taste and is quite genre-specific. The only real guideline is that moderation is key when it comes to adding reverb to multiple tracks.

Mastering Effects

Compression and Equalization Revisited

The master track details view also includes three additional processing slots. Frankly, their placement in relationship to the master echo and reverb effects is a bit misleading, if not downright confusing, as they appear to follow these effects in series when in fact they process the entire mix—and all of the instruments within—as a whole, both the reverb and echo output and any signals coming from the tracks that arrive "dry," without passing through the reverb and echo.

Figure 6-3
Along with EQ and compression, you can also apply one of GarageBand's other effects to your master output via the Master Track Info window.

The purpose of these effects is to put the final sheen on your song, a process that professional engineers refer to as *mastering*. To get a feel for how this process works, experiment with the master track presets available in each of the categories. For example, the Hip Hop Deep Thump preset emphasizes the bass while adding a fair amount of compression to your mix, whereas the Jazz Club preset adds a touch of emphasis to the treble frequencies and moderately compresses the final result.

The first processor is user-selectable, as with the individual track effects. You can insert any of the above-described effects as the first processor in this chain. It's noteworthy that none of the factory mastering presets make use of this additional processor. Why? Because slapping a phaser or tremolo or auto-wah on an entire track sounds kinda *wrong*—unless, of course, you're making extremely experimental music, in which case you're probably not following very many engineering guidelines in the first place.

That said, the following two processors, equalization and compression respectively, are a great way to give your tracks a polished, professional sound. For example, you might find that your overall song is a trifle bass-heavy because of the drum loops and bass sounds you've chosen. At this point, you can do one of two things: go back to your mix and tinker further with the tracks in question (the preferable option, in my opinion) or activate the EQ processor and attenuate the bass frequencies slightly.

Alternatively, after burning your track to CD and playing it on a few different systems, you may find that your monitoring system is a trifle bright, thus making your mix sound somewhat dull in the high frequencies on other systems. To compensate, you'd want to apply the EQ again, this time boosting the treble slightly and perhaps enhancing the upper mid frequencies a touch. As with all equalization, subtlety and restraint will help you achieve the most natural results.

The compressor is another way to give your mixes that ready-for-radio sound. If you're making dance music or hip-hop, you may find your songs have a bit too much low-frequency energy. In this case, you'd use the EQ to attenuate the bass ever so slightly, then add a fair amount of compression to give the track a punchy, even sound.

Since the factory mastering presets are so darn good, I'd recommend using one of them as a starting point for your final polishing, then fine-tune the individual processors to get the most out of your mix. When selecting a mastering preset, don't limit yourself to the ones that are specific to your genre. Try them all. You may find that a classical or jazz preset is better suited to your trance or house opus than one of the dance presets, so rely on your ears when making these selections.

Additionally, if you're using a preset-based approach, keep in mind that the master presets also include settings for your global echo and reverb units, so you may have to go back and restore these to *your* preferred settings. Not a big deal, but something to be aware of as you put the finishing touches on your music.

Chapter 7
Mixing

Once you've selected and arranged the loops, keyboard parts, and recorded instruments for your masterpiece, you'll be faced with another aspect of the joyous craft of music-making: mixing. Congratulations, you've just entered the world of audio engineering—a parallel universe where art and science intermingle and even the experts can't agree on a universal approach to the task.

Due to CPU performance considerations, most GarageBand compositions tend to contain between eight and twenty tracks total. If you're lucky enough to have a top-of-the-line dual G5 system, you may be able to eke out a few more tracks for embellishment, but that's the exception—not the rule—in most cases.

In this chapter, we'll discuss the essential concepts behind mixing your tracks to form a cohesive whole, and also offer some tips and tricks for troubleshooting and optimizing your mixes.

Anatomy of a Mix

A common lineup for a pop, rock, or dance track will go something like this: one or two tracks for drums and percussion, a bass track, one or two rhythmic instrument tracks like guitar or synth, a melody lead line or two (synth, guitar, or other recorded instrument), lead vocals, harmony vocals, and perhaps a sound effect or cymbal crash for dramatic emphasis during certain passages. That's about five to ten tracks, each needing its own space in the final mix. Each track needs to be heard clearly, and none of them should overpower the others.

Drums

When you're building a house, you begin with a strong and solid foundation. In music, the drum and percussion elements form the foundation for your mix. When you begin mixing, mute or turn the levels down on *all* other instruments and start with your drum and percussion loops.

Now, listen closely. Are all of the elements in each loop crisp and clear? Is the timing and/or feel of each loop complementing the other elements?

If the *sound* of the combined elements is satisfying, then focus on the groove. It's important to avoid the sound of flamming—that is, two drums that hit on the same beat, but at slightly different times, thus sounding somewhat sloppy. Common causes of flamming include inaccurate playing by a live drummer or percussionist, different quantization resolutions between loops, and loops that are not perfectly aligned at their start points.

If you're working with MIDI-based Apple Loops, you may be able to realign the grooves by setting identical Fix Timing (quantization) amounts for both loops. You might also want to revisit some of the loop blending techniques outlined in the Loops and MIDI chapters. If none of those approaches works, you may need to replace one of the drum loops with another that fits your groove more appropriately. Snipping a single drum hit out of an audio loop and moving it backward or forward slightly in time is a lot of work, but once in a while it may be the best solution.

Once your grooves are aligned, examine the relationships in the low end of the combined loops, specifically the kick drums. All too often, combining kick drum patterns will create muddiness in the low-frequency range. If this is the case, decide which drum loop will be your dominant pattern, then judiciously apply the bass reduction filter to the secondary loop, thus minimizing its kick drum pattern and allowing the other to take precedence.

Once the drums and percussion are aligned, carefully balance the levels of each loop, keeping an eye on the meters for each track *and* the master meter. At this point, it's best to keep the master meters just below the yellow segments. As you add more instrumentation, the overall volume will increase, so you want to start your mix conservatively and leave room to grow.

Bass

Now it's time to add the bass. This can be somewhat tricky. If the bass is too loud, it will overwhelm the frequency range of the kick drum. If it's too quiet, it will get lost in the mix.

GarageBand comes with a huge assortment of bass loops—including acoustic, electric, and synth types. Some are loaded with subsonic bombast; others are punchier in the midrange. Each type has its merits, so it's important to determine what your track needs sonically.

Depending on the type of loop you've chosen—or the bass part you've recorded via MIDI or audio—your options for blending differ. When you unmute, or raise the level of, your bass line, do so slowly, listening closely to how it interacts with the kick drum hits. If it fits nicely, you're in luck. Just set it and move on.

If there's a sonic conflict of some sort, first determine whether there's too much or too little low-end energy in the bass. In either case, you have several options for remedy.

If you're using a software instrument, try adjusting the various synthesis parameters to customize your bass sound. Adjusting the cutoff frequency will brighten or dull the bass sound, allowing it to fit into the mix better. If the bass seems to be taking up too much space, another approach may be to shorten the decay or release time of the bass synth, making it more percussive as well as shortening its duration.

Another possible fix for boomy MIDI bass lines is to take the part up an octave by setting the transposition slider to 12, then further adjusting the parameters on the software instrument.

If you're using recorded audio or a loop for your bass part, you have several options for tweaking the sound. The bass and treble reduction effects will go a long way toward shaping the sound of an electric bass. Equalization is another option, though I prefer the reduction effects in my mixes for subtle sculpting tasks. A third option is the automatic filter effect, with the intensity control set to "off" so as not to create unwanted level shifts.

Once you've tailored the sound of the bass, try adding a touch of compression, as this will give the overall texture a bit more prominence. From there, set your final levels in relationship to the drums, again keeping an eye on your master meter and avoiding peaks in the red.

Now save your song, take a short break, and give your ears a little rest.

Rhythmic and Chordal Instruments

Now you're ready to add the chordal and rhythmic instruments, which may include guitar, electric piano, organ, and/or percolating synth bits.

Start by slowly raising one of these elements until it complements your bass and drum groove. Now examine the sound critically. Are the effects you've applied to the track suitably placed, or are they overwhelming the sound? Make adjustments in small increments rather than broad strokes. Sometimes backing off a bit on the echo or reverb will make all the difference. Other times, a touch of bass/treble reduction or EQ will do the trick. The secret here is subtlety, because you want

TEARS FOR EARS: Ear fatigue is a real phenomenon and can affect the decisions you make when working on a track. As you mix, be sure to take breaks every hour or so. Save your composition and go for a walk, make some coffee or food (alcohol can affect your mix judgment, so beware), or do some studio housekeeping. Whatever you do, make sure you're giving your ears a break and allowing yourself the time to regain your perspective. This break should be a minimum of 5–10 minutes. Take as long as you need, but give yourself a little time away from the piece. When you return to it, you may be surprised at how your impressions have changed.

to retain the unique tonal characteristics of your instrumental passage while blending it with the overall mix.

If you have multiple rhythmic parts, now's the time to experiment with panning. Try moving a rhythm guitar slightly to the left and an electric piano comp an equal amount to the right. Or try the same approach with two percussive synthesizer parts. Often, this technique will open up your mix, making it more spacious and allowing each instrument room to breathe. When all your parts are straight up the middle, you're practically mixing in mono! Giving each instrument a position in the stereo field is a classic way to add interest and avoid clutter.

At this point, your basic mix should be balanced, with each instrument occupying its own frequency range and position in the stereo field. If this isn't happening, go back and make incremental adjustments as needed. Remember: Less is more.

Vocals and Lead Instruments

Once the essentials are in place, it's time to add your focal musical parts, such as lead vocals or guitar and synth hooks.

The highlighted parts of your composition should be up front and center. Begin by adding a touch of compression to these parts so that any dynamic variations in the performance don't cause them to get lost in the mix.

If it's a vocal that serves as the focus for your song, decide whether you want it to be intimate and direct or big and dramatic. Either approach is totally valid, it just depends on the context of your music. If in doubt, fire up your copy of iTunes and check out some of your favorite tracks in the mix's genre. How are the highlighted elements treated in those tracks?

Once you've made your decisions, return to your vocal or lead. If you're going for an intimate, up-front sound, then go easy on the effects, instead relying on compression and EQ for emphasis. Sometimes a whisper of overdrive will lend a voice some added edge, bringing it to the forefront without overwhelming the other elements.

On the other hand, if you want the lead parts to shimmer and swim in the mix, try applying some rhythmic echo, perhaps with a dotted-eighth-note or quarter-note delay time. Beware of the temptation to add too much reverb to a vocal. Even with the best reverb algorithms, this effect can often make an otherwise excellent mix sound cheesy and amateurish.

Go over your levels one more time, making sure that there are no peaks or overloading. Tweak levels as needed.

Sound Effects and Cymbal Crashes

By now, your mix should be sounding balanced and nearing completion. If you have any transitional sound effects or cymbal crashes that set off the choruses or breakdowns, it's time to add them.

Using your EQ and effects knowledge, add processing as needed. Even though these elements are there to add spice and drama to your composition, they should always be placed in relationship to the other parts. Overly loud cymbal crashes or exotic sound bites will cheapen a good mix. Conversely, if these parts are too quiet, they merely get lost without adding the desired impact.

If everything is sounding good at this point, save your song and take a long break. If you have time, come back to the song a day later, so that you return to your mix with refreshed ears and new perspective.

Finishing Touches

When you come back to your mix, listen to it from start to finish once before re-suming work. It may also be a good idea to create a copy of your original mix, giv-ing the next version a slightly different name or adding a version number to the filename. This way, if you make changes that lead you away from your goal, you can always revert to the last good mix as a backup.

After you've made any needed revisions to your previous mix, it's time to add the final polish. First, go though each track and adjust effects amounts as needed. Then tweak your levels and panning to maximize your blend and avoid peak overloads.

Now listen closely. Are the vocals and/or leads prominent throughout the mix? If not, you may wish to add a bit of level automation to these tracks. Click on the track volume display button (the downward arrow next to the solo and mute buttons) and locate the position in your song that requires a level change. Click on the line, adding automation points just before and after the area that you want to boost or lower. This will enable you to return to the original levels quickly if you make a mis-take or revise your decisions at a later date.

When adding automation, it's very important to make very small, incremental changes. A boost of 3dB is roughly equivalent to doubling the volume of a track, due to the logarithmic nature of sound and acoustics. If a vocal needs a bit more pres-ence during the chorus of your song, just nudge it up a whisker. You'll probably be surprised at the difference even a tiny change can make.

Conversely, you can add excitement by fading in musical parts over the course of several measures rather than simply starting and ending at precise bar lengths. If you're still unfamiliar with GarageBand's automation tools, set aside some time to experiment with them. Volume changes are a crucial tool in a producer's arsenal for

Figure 7-1
Volume automation is a great way to tame an overly dynamic per-formance. Note the automation "anchor points" just before and after the level change.

adding interest to a mix. You can easily program fade-ins and fade-outs by activating the track volume display in the track header and setting automation points. You can find this in the GarageBand Help in the "Mixing your song" section, under "Adding and adjusting control points."

When your mix reaches the point of completion, it's a good idea to burn an audio CD—or export the song to your iPod—and try it on different systems, especially if your studio is equipped with small or semi-pro monitors. Play the mix in your car, on a boom box, and on a portable personal stereo (using consumer-grade headphones). If it sounds balanced and even on all of these systems, you're probably good to go. If not, take notes and make subtle adjustments when you return to your studio.

Alternatively, if you're working on a laptop, you could get a cassette adapter and run the output of your laptop directly into your car or home stereo, making *minute* tweaks to optimize it for different systems. Just make sure that your car-optimized version still sounds good on other systems. Once the mix checks out on a variety of listening platforms, you're done! Export the mix to iTunes and share your masterpiece with the world.

One last thought on the final polishing phase: It's easy to get lost in the mixing process or even let your personal insecurities get in the way of completing the work. Don't undermine your talents by leaving work unfinished. Even if you decide it's not your "best" song, or you want to move on to the next glittering jewel that your muse has provided, take the time to finish the project. Only by *completing* each project can you develop the experience needed to make the next one better. I know too many truly talented musicians who subsist in "demo mode." Regrettably, by not completing their ideas, they never find the path to growth, which lies in finishing each song and growing from these experiences. If nothing more, when a client or record label asks to hear more of your work, you'll have additional tracks to play for them.

Ten Essential Mixing Tips and Techniques

Good Monitoring Tools

The secret to making recordings that sound great on a variety of systems lies in having flat monitor speakers. By "flat," I mean that the speakers must have a balanced frequency spectrum from the lows to the highs. "Good-sounding" consumer-oriented audio monitors aren't necessarily the most honest ones.

Why? Because if your monitors have a pronounced bass response, you may overcompensate by under-emphasizing the lows, or worse yet, reducing them—resulting in a mix that's the acoustic inverse of your monitoring system. Conversely, if your monitors have a sizzling high-frequency response, you may react by reducing the treble, thus creating a mix that sounds dull or muted on other systems.

By relying on honest, flat monitors, you ensure that what you hear is accurate and you can make EQ and mix decisions that are free of built-in bias. Since there are so many options for monitors in a wide variety of price ranges, I recommend that you set a price point for your speakers, do a bit of online research, then proceed to your favorite music store and work with a knowledgeable salesperson to determine which model best suits your budget and needs. Sadly, computer speakers are generally *not* recommended, as they're designed to sound "good," not honest, and are often slightly hyped for PC gamers.

Versioning

A time-tested secret of many computer-based musicians and producers is the process of *versioning*. Savvy engineers know that sometimes, in the heat of creative passion, we all make decisions that lead us *away* from a balanced recording. Versioning allows us the luxury of being able to return to an earlier version that we know sounds good and resume work from that point. Sort of like an infinite undo function.

Here's how to do it: When you start a new song, create a folder with that song's name and place your initial version inside that folder. Every time you make considerable changes to your composition, re-save it with a slightly different name to the same folder. I use a numbering system, incrementing the version number in the filename every time I update a composition. If I make a wrong turn as I continue work, I just revert to the last decent mix.

Since GarageBand saves all of the associated audio files within its song packages, this approach can eat up drive space at an alarming rate. If you find yourself running out of room on your hard drive, just delete the versions of the song that you're sure you no longer need.

The Eight-Bar Rule

Here's an arrangement trick that will help keep your compositions interesting, regardless of the genre. It works best with popular forms of music in 4/4 time, but can be applied to any style with good results.

If you examine the structure of your favorite songs, you'll probably notice that something about the arrangement changes every four to eight bars, usually eight. Sometimes it's the addition or subtraction of an instrument or riff. Other times it's the introduction of an entirely new passage, like a chorus or verse. As long as you keep the arrangement in motion by shifting the elements every eight bars, you'll retain your audience's interest over the course of the song.

The secret lies in walking the fine line between subtle and severe. Huge changes are fine for a breakdown or dramatic chorus, but can be disorienting if they occur too frequently. Too many subtle changes can get lost in the context of your mix, thus defeating the purpose of this technique.

It may take a bit of experimentation, but once you get the hang of it, you'll see why this approach is a staple of remixers and pop producers.

The Solo Trap

One of the biggest mistakes that fledgling producers and engineers make is soloing an instrument to apply EQ or adjust effects while they're mixing.

Why is this a mistake? Well, when you're mixing, you're methodically blending the levels and frequency ranges of your instruments *in relationship to each other*. If you solo an instrument to make these changes, you're adjusting the balance out of context.

Often, the individual components of a good mix may sound odd when soloed. This is because their effects and EQs were applied to make them work holistically with the other elements.

Bottom line? Use the solo button to critically examine an individual part for recording errors or flubbed notes, *not* to audition equalization or effects outside the context of your mix.

Good Housekeeping: Maximizing Your CPU

While GarageBand is an incredibly powerful composition tool for musicians of all levels, many of its Software Instrument presets and Apple Loops contain added effects to enhance their sound.

Each of these effects eats up CPU resources. Some effects eat up more CPU time than others, so if you rely extensively on loops, it's a good idea to occasionally check the information panel's details view whenever you add a software instrument or loop to your arrangement. Try deactivating certain effects and see if the results negatively impact the sound. If there's not much change, then leave them off so they don't unnecessarily consume valuable resources.

Additionally, you may wish to convert your Software Instrument loops to Real Instrument loops whenever possible. The conversion technique is described in the Loops chapter of this book.

Track Freezing

Another great way to make the most of your resources is to steal a page from Emagic's (and Apple's) flagship production environment, Logic, and "freeze" tracks that contain extensive effects processing. While Logic has the advantage of making the process a one-click affair, you can still accomplish the task within GarageBand if you're willing to spend a bit of time on it.

What freezing does is take a Software Instrument MIDI track or heavily processed audio track and render it as a separate audio file. The result is then re-imported into a new track while the old track—and its associate processing—is muted, thus conserving resources.

1) Begin by determining your song's *final* BPM. Once you freeze your track(s), you won't be able to change tempo unless you revert to the original sequence and re-freeze the tracks.
2) Solo the track you want to freeze, muting the echo and reverb send effects, since you can reapply these later.
3) Now export your GarageBand song to iTunes. Since all tracks are muted except for your soloed part, your rendered audio file will consist of just the track you want to freeze.
4) Open iTunes and find your frozen track. If you can't find it immediately, sort your iTunes library by "date created" or "date modified." This will bring your track to the top of the playlist.
5) Highlight your frozen track in iTunes and press Command+R. iTunes will then find and open the folder on your system where the frozen track resides. Drag the file to your desktop and rename it something recognizable so you can keep track of it.
6) Now drag your newly frozen track from the desktop to an empty area in Garage-Band's Timeline area. This will automagically create a new track that contains the frozen audio.
7) Finally, save your song. GarageBand will duplicate your frozen track in the song's ".band" file, allowing you to dispose of your source AIFF file if you like.

Repeat as needed with any other tracks that make use of extensive processing. The more tracks you freeze, the lighter the load on your CPU. You can still rearrange your frozen tracks within your song using the audio editor and split commands.

Effects Tips

GarageBand's extraordinary arsenal of effects is a dual-edged sword. Applied judiciously with a tasteful ear, they can add a truly professional sheen to your mixes. Slap 'em indiscriminately on all your tracks and you can quickly end up with a muddy mess. While there aren't many hard-and-fast rules for where and when to apply effects processors to your instruments, here are some basic guidelines.

Reverb. If you use GarageBand's global reverb, apply the reverb to only one or two select instruments in a mix to highlight them. If you apply reverb to too many tracks simultaneously, you'll end up with that "stadium roar effect." That is, the processed tracks will create a wash of sound like a live concert. While this can be a neat trick for an intro or middle section of a song, it will obscure sonic detail if applied to an entire song. Use reverb with restraint and it will serve you well.

Echo. If you want to add a touch of depth to a vocal or highlighted instrument, consider applying synchronized echo instead of reverb. When your echo repeats are synchronized with your song tempo, they integrate more smoothly into the overall mix while still adding motion and ambience to the effected instruments.

If you like syncopated rhythms, try setting the delay time to dotted eighth-notes or dotted quarter-notes and apply this echo to selected percussive instruments. The rolling nature of the resulting rhythm will add interest to even the most mundane groove.

Modulation Effects. Chorus, phaser, filter, and flange effects are a terrific way to add animation and depth to certain tracks, and work well on nearly all types of signals. However, as with reverb, if you add modulation effects to more than one or two tracks in a mix, you may end up with too much motion and lose definition and detail in your overall blend. Additionally, you might also create phantom overloads in your gain structure as the peaks of your modulated effects cross, emphasizing certain frequency ranges as they move through them. If this occurs, systematically mute suspect tracks until the problem disappears, then go back and adjust the effects on the problem track.

Distortion, Bitcrushing, Overdrive, and Amp Simulation. Mangling certain signals can be a useful approach to adding aggression and power to specific parts. Used conservatively, these effects are also handy for imparting a warm, organic quality to otherwise dry tracks. Applying moderate amounts of overdrive or bitcrushing to drum and percussion loops will give them a gritty edge. Bass lines can get a jolt of energy from a touch of distortion, allowing them to better cut through a mix. And of course, that classic industrial voice effect that Ministry and Skinny Puppy made so popular in the '80s can be achieved by adding an amp simulator or distortion to a vocal.

EQ in Moderation

A common pitfall for many novice producers lies in the application of EQ to every track in a mix. As a rule of thumb, try to limit EQ to only the tracks that truly require adjustment. More often than not, you can give an instrument more space by paying closer attention to its level and panning, rather than just boosting the high, mid, or low frequencies.

Another issue can arise when musicians use extensive EQ for emphasizing frequencies instead of reducing them. For one thing, boosting frequencies often leads to an overall level increase in your signal, which can damage your carefully planned gain structure and add distortion or clipping to your mix. Rather than raising the level of desired frequencies, try cutting the level of *undesired* frequencies. This is one of the reasons that I tend to rely on the bass and treble reduction tools and software instrument parameters, as opposed to EQ. More often than not, shaving off a bit of low-frequency information will allow an instrument to sit better in a mix and take up less sonic space, giving the other instruments more breathing room.

Ersatz Automation

Considering that it's a fifty-dollar application, it's remarkable that GarageBand offers track automation. Unfortunately, it's strictly for volume control of each track. Even so, there's a workaround that allows you to kinda-sorta automate your effects and panning, within reason.

If you want a track in your song to gradually include processing like flanging or distortion, you can accomplish the effect by crossfading between two versions of the track—one with effects and one without. Simply create a new track, preferably adjacent to the track you want to process so that you can easily view both tracks at once. Now copy the audio or loop to this new track and apply your effects as desired.

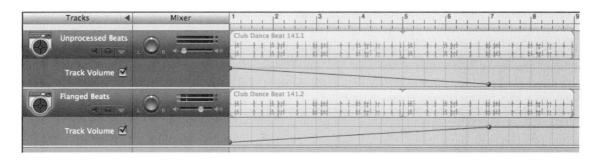

From there, it's a simple matter to activate track volume automation and draw a crossfade—fade one track out while the other track fades in—at the desired points. Alternatively, if you want an abrupt transition between the two tracks, use the split function (command+T) and delete the audio from one track or the other as needed to create the effect you're after.

Figure 7-2
By crossfading between two tracks—one with effects and one without—you can simulate true effects automation.

Mistakes Are Good

Over the years, some of my favorite mix tricks have been discovered entirely by accident—or by doing things the "wrong" way. While this chapter has outlined quite a few traditional guidelines for approaching a mix, there's always room for experimentation.

Here's a trick for giving yourself a new perspective on a mix. Begin by making a copy of your song file and give it a new name, like "mysong_experiment.band." Then open the new file and, *before you play the song,* open each track's details view and randomly make changes to it without listening to the results.

Switch software instruments. Change effects settings or apply entirely new effects. Chop up parts using the techniques described in the Loop and Audio chapters. But be sure you do all of this tinkering *without* listening as you work.

Once you've made a fair number of changes, save your copied file, then go back and listen to the changes. If you're lucky, you might stumble upon an interesting effect or sound that you otherwise would not have created had you been "thinking" about what you were doing.

In certain situations, chaos can be a friend rather than an enemy. The secret lies in knowing how to apply randomization in a controlled fashion. Experiment! Take chances! Knowing the rules is always the first step toward *knowing how to break them*.

Troubleshooting Your Mixes

Challenge: None of the original tracks are clipping, but the master outputs are in the red and/or there's distortion in the final output.

Solutions: The answer lies somewhere within your overall gain structure. Perhaps you're overloading a track by using an effect like overdrive, distortion, or amp simulation, which is changing the gain. Alternatively, the problem may lie in a combination of instruments emphasizing certain frequency ranges (this often happens when mixing drum loops with a lot of low-frequency energy). Try tweaking your effects settings and lowering the level of every track slightly while maintaining the balance of your mix, or apply a little bass reduction effect to one or more of your loops.

Finally, some modulation effects like flangers, choruses, and phasers can create dynamic peaks within a signal as they move through various frequency ranges. If this is the case, pull back slightly on the resonance or feedback parameters of the suspect effects and see if that helps.

Challenge: The bass elements are muddy and/or boomy.

Solution: Is the kick drum competing with the bass line? If so, readjust the balance and/or tuning of these elements. Do other tracks contain unnecessary low-frequency information? Try rolling off some of the lows on these tracks—using EQ or the bass reducer—to keep the emphasis on the kick and bass line.

Challenge: Shrill or piercing high frequencies in the mix.

Solution: Do your drum loops have excessive or harsh hi-hats and cymbals? Consider adjusting the EQ on these tracks or applying a treble reducer to tame the troublesome frequencies. Have you applied too much EQ boost to the treble frequencies in certain elements? Focus on the upper and midranges of these tracks and minimize where necessary.

Challenge: Mixes don't translate to a range of listening environments (car stereos, portable stereos, boom boxes).

Solution: Do your monitors have a relatively flat frequency response? Have you applied additional EQ to your amplification system? Are you using a subwoofer to enhance or exaggerate the bass in your monitoring environment? Are you mixing on headphones instead of using professional-grade speakers? Each of the above approaches can compromise your listening environment, creating undesirable emphasis in certain frequency ranges.

Always try to listen to your mixes on neutral-sounding, professional-quality monitors—as much as your budget will allow. Then double-check the mixes on a variety of consumer-grade systems.

Challenge: Mixes sound flat or lifeless.

Solution: Are your levels set correctly? Setting your track levels too low will sometimes compromise your bit-depth, resulting in inadequate resolution, which translates to a decrease in dynamic range.

Have you applied additional effects to enhance or add ambience to specific elements? If not, consider spicing up a few tracks with effects to highlight important parts. Alternatively, have you applied too much compression to your tracks or to the whole mix? Restraining the dynamics of too many parts can often lead to an overall decrease in energy.

Finally, are there too many elements playing at the same time? While a wall of sound can be useful for creating tension and drama, it can also dull the overall intensity of a song. Consider revising the arrangement in order to highlight transitions and critical melodies and loops.

Challenge: The mix suffers from a lack of definition. Individual instruments are getting lost or washed out.

Solutions: Are there too many effects in place? Are the reverb decays too long? Often, gratuitous use of effects can cause the mix to lose its crispness and presence. Another area to consider is the amount of midrange and lower midrange in your individual tracks. Try modifying several tracks with EQ or bass/treble reduction, either by lowering the lows and mids or by subtly emphasizing the highs.

Challenge: Balance of instruments is erratic. Tracks suddenly change volume during a mix.

Solution: If certain elements, such as a vocal performance or solo instrument, "jump out" during certain passages, consider applying compression or limiting to modify the dynamic range of the sample or loop. Or instead, try using volume automation to lower the volume of the offending track in problematic areas.

Challenge: There's a lack of stereo width in the mix.

Solution: Double-check each track's panning. Try placing supporting elements further apart in the stereo field. Apply spatial stereo effects like reverb and/or chorus to instruments like pads and strings. Add synchronized delay to rhythmic parts and pan as needed.

Challenge: Mix is boring.

Solution: Revisit your arrangement and see if you're applying the eight-bar rule (explained earlier in this chapter) to your elements. Another handy trick is to apply the automatic filter effect—with a long, slow sweep that repeats over four or more measures (sixteen or more beats)—to a highlighted track. This will give the impression of moving the selected instrument into and out of the mix, drawing the listeners' ears to it.

Challenge: Mix doesn't sound polished.

Solution: Even the most well-thought-out mixes can sometimes sound under-produced in comparison to commercial releases. The secret here lies in the mastering process. Experiment with using some of the Master Track presets, even if the preset name doesn't necessarily match the style of music you're making. The EQ and compression settings in one of these presets may be exactly what your mix needs. Good engineers know that mastering is the secret to finalizing an already complete mix.

Challenge: All of these considerations are really tedious and difficult to integrate into my approach to recording.

Solution: Don't forget to have fun. This *is* music, after all.

Chapter 8
Expanding GarageBand

After working with GarageBand for a while, you may start to feel the need to upgrade. If your music is primarily loop-based, you'll be happy to learn there's an ever-expanding assortment of developers working on libraries in the Apple Loop format. If MIDI is your weapon of choice, you may want to consider adding a new synth or two to GarageBand's already formidable arsenal. If you work with audio and/or "traditional" instruments and you want more exotic sound processing tools, then plug-in effects are the way to go.

In this chapter, we'll cover some of the more interesting options available as of mid-2004, with a focus on affordability as well as flexibility—first the plug-in synths and effects, then loop libraries, and finally some other useful accessories.

Considering the scope and number of effects and software instruments that Garage-Band ships with and how affordable the program is, Apple could have been forgiven for making GarageBand a closed system. So it's a welcome surprise that they included full support for their Audio Unit plug-in format. This support allows users to add third-party effects and software synthesizers to GarageBand, just as they would when working with any professional-grade sequencing tool.

Of course, when you stop to consider that GarageBand is practically free, hot-rodding it with a three-hundred-dollar softsynth or a thousand-dollar effects package may seem like adding nitrous injectors to a scooter. Audio Unit compatibility also allows you to take advantage of the multitude of freeware plug-ins available for download on the Web. Since there are literally hundreds of Audio Unit plug-ins available at the time of this writing, we don't have room in this book for descriptions of all of them. If you want to research your commercial plug-in options, I strongly recommend checking out Jim Aikin's *Software Synthesizers* book, also available from Backbeat Books. While the focus of that tome is on software instruments rather than effects, it's an excellent way to discover what's out there and determine whether you should add more plug-ins to GarageBand.

To save you some time, we've done a thorough assessment of cost-effective Garage-Band add-ons. Many of these plug-ins are also located on the included CD-ROM, so if you're intrigued, just pop in the CD and check them out.

Freeware Synth Plug-Ins

Alphakanal

If it's analog-style synthesis you're after, and if you have some familiarity with sound programming basics, you'll definitely be interested in Alphakanal's buzZer2 softsynth. Sporting two oscillators, two multimode resonant filters (be sure to check out the vowel formant mode—it's outstanding), three envelopes, and a dedicated multi-waveform LFO for each oscillator, filter, and amplifier, buzZer2 is a surprisingly powerful little plug. While not as straightforward for novices as the synths in GarageBand, it's a terrific introduction to the world of subtractive synthesis.

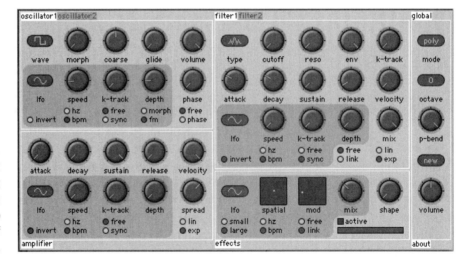

Figure 8-1
Alphakanal's buzZer2 is a powerful analog synth emulation with two oscillators, two filters, and an array of modulation options.

Expert Sleepers

The developers behind the humorously named Expert Sleepers line of plug-ins have delivered not one but two nifty freeware plug-in synths that are compatible with GarageBand: Crossfade Loop Synth and Additive Synth. While both are included on the CD, they are donationware, *not* freeware. This means that it's okay to use their tools in your music, but if you do so with regularity, you're encouraged to pay for the software, if only for karmic reasons.

Crossfade Loop Synth is a super-simple sampler that can host a single sampled audio file in either AIFF, WAV, or SD2 format. The selected file is mapped across your entire keyboard so that you can play it melodically or rhythmically. Once the sample is in memory, you can further tweak it via a multimode resonant filter and a couple of basic envelopes. Frankly, for quick-and-dirty sampling, I even use this plug inside professional sequencers like Logic. It's that handy.

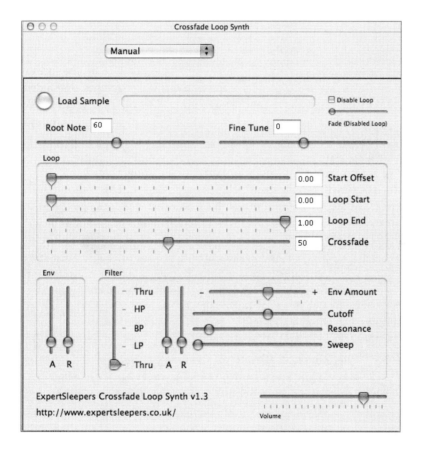

Figure 8-2
With support for multiple audio formats, filters and basic envelope tools, Crossfade Loop Synth is the perfect introduction to sampling.

With direct control over the volumes of the first eight frequencies in the harmonic series and a simple attack-release envelope, Additive Synth is a wonderful first step into the complex world of additive synthesis. With this synth plug-in you can easily create chime and organ-like sounds that sound wonderful in a variety of contexts.

Figure 8-3
Additive Synth offers
control over the
volume of the first
eight harmonics and a
simple attack-release
envelope.

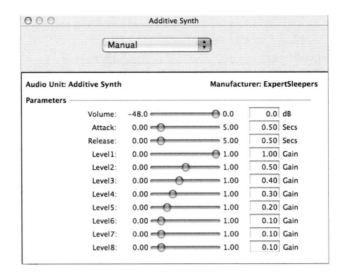

Green Oak Software

If you've got processor headroom to spare and a real jones for hardcore synthesis tools, then be sure to install Green Oak Software's Crystal. This softsynth is the toast of the freeware plug-in community, with a feature array that can go toe-to-toe with some of the better commercial synths out there. The synthesis modes include both subtractive and FM, and there are plenty of modulation options. Suffice to say, if Absynth and Reaktor are out of your price range, Crystal is a decent substitute—and that's saying a *lot*. The only real consideration is that a synth this powerful requires a hefty chunk of CPU and RAM. G5 users will be in heaven. G3 and G4 users may be a trifle frustrated.

Glaresoft iDrum

While it's not a freeware plug-in, at a price of $50 (US), Glaresoft's iDrum definitely deserves a mention if you're looking to create custom beats in GarageBand. Unlike many other software drum machines, iDrum doesn't limit you to a set number of drum channels. If you run out of tracks, just use the pull-down and add another, then assign the sample of your choice. Each track offers a useful array of editing functions for customizing your samples, including volume, pan, pitch, sample decay, highpass and lowpass filters, and bit-depth (adjustable from 4-bit to 32-bit). There are even two choke groups for cutting off hi-hats, triangles, toms, and so forth. For playing

TEMPO CALCULATIONS: If you're working with an echo effect that's not automagically synchronized to GarageBand's tempo, you can still calculate the delay time in milliseconds for quarter-notes with this simple equation: 60,000 divided by BPM. The result will give you the exact number of milliseconds per beat. For instance, at 120 BPM, each quarter-note lasts for 60,000/120, or 500ms (½ second). For half-note values, multiply the result by two. For eighth-note delays, divide the result by two, and so forth.

drum patterns and fills directly from a keyboard controller, each drum channel can be mapped to its own MIDI note number as well.

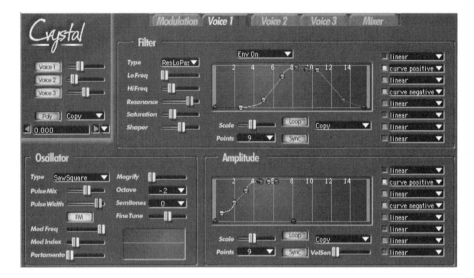

Figure 8-4
Crystal may be a bit CPU-hungry, but that's because it's one of the most powerful free-ware synth plug-ins available. Dig the multistage envelopes!

Figure 8-5
Prefer making your beats with the tried-and-true TR-style interface popularized by Roland? At only fifty bucks, iDrum is the way to go.

The drum samples that come with iDrum are grouped into four categories: kicks, snares, hats, and perc, the latter including everything from claves to tablas. There are over a hundred preset kits to choose from, covering pretty much every modern electronica genre with aplomb aplenty.

Groove creation is pattern-style, and there are 99 pattern slots available. These can be strung into songs in real time, using a "switch-pattern-as-the-grooves-play" approach. While this is definitely not my first choice for intuitive programming, it's not unprecedented either. Your mileage may vary.

For OS X users of all types, iDrum is a terrific value. Don't believe me? Check out the fully functional 30-day demo on the CD and see for yourself.

Freeware Effects

Expert Sleepers

As if their synth plugs weren't enough, Expert Sleepers have also generously created several useful donationware Audio Unit effects that sound terrific and work well in GarageBand. Their Phaser plug-in is sonically similar to GarageBand's but with additional adjustable parameters including minimum and maximum sweep ranges, intensity, and stereo spread.

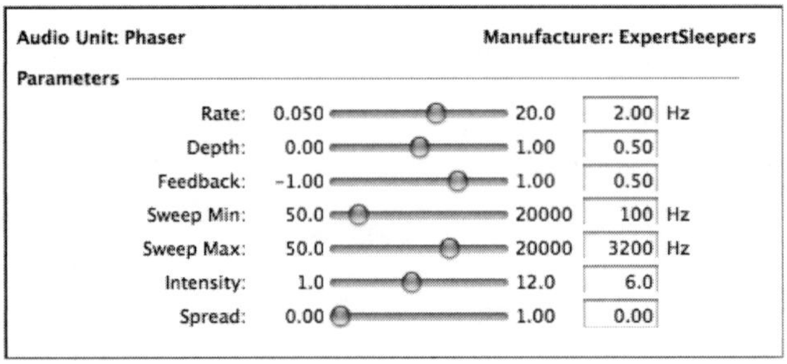

Figure 8-6
Want more control over your phasing effects than GarageBand delivers? Try Expert Sleepers' nifty Phaser plug-in. It's on the CD-ROM.

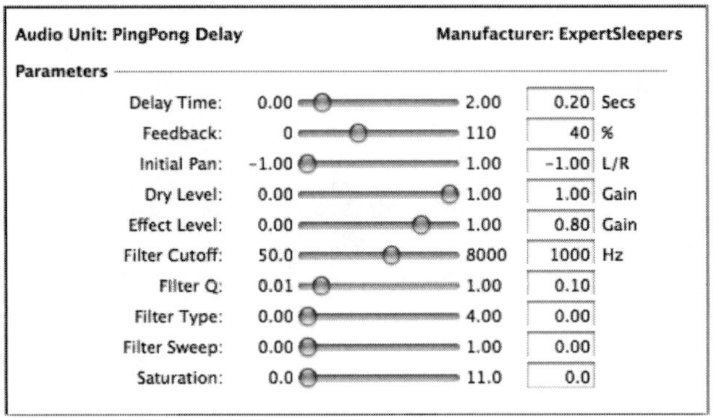

Audio Unit: Phaser			Manufacturer: ExpertSleepers
Parameters			
Rate:	0.050	20.0	2.00 Hz
Depth:	0.00	1.00	0.50
Feedback:	-1.00	1.00	0.50
Sweep Min:	50.0	20000	100 Hz
Sweep Max:	50.0	20000	3200 Hz
Intensity:	1.0	12.0	6.0
Spread:	0.00	1.00	0.00

Figure 8-7
If you're prepared to do the math necessary to synchronize your delay times, PingPong Delay will give you a lot of control over your echo effects.

Audio Unit: PingPong Delay			Manufacturer: ExpertSleepers
Parameters			
Delay Time:	0.00	2.00	0.20 Secs
Feedback:	0	110	40 %
Initial Pan:	-1.00	1.00	-1.00 L/R
Dry Level:	0.00	1.00	1.00 Gain
Effect Level:	0.00	1.00	0.80 Gain
Filter Cutoff:	50.0	8000	1000 Hz
Filter Q:	0.01	1.00	0.10
Filter Type:	0.00	4.00	0.00
Filter Sweep:	0.00	1.00	0.00
Saturation:	0.0	11.0	0.0

The PingPong Delay is a stereo echo that bounces the delayed signal around the left and right outputs. It includes swept resonant filters and a saturation control that delivers overdrive-like effects. Unlike GarageBand's delays, you'll need to set your delay time in milliseconds, since this effect is not automatically synchronized to tempo.

The Multitap Delay takes the PingPong Delay's bid and raises it by two, providing *four* independent delays, each with its own time, feedback, and pan controls. As with the PingPong version, there are ample filtering tools and a saturation control. Again, you'll need to calculate your own delay times if you want to synchronize the tempo.

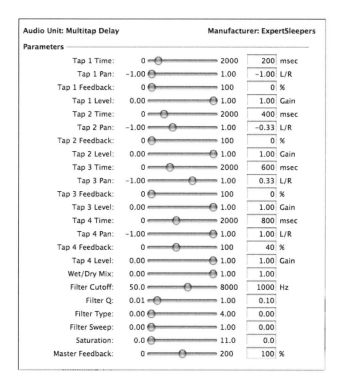

Figure 8-8
Two delays not enough? Try four, each with its own filter and pan controls.

Ohm Force

Ohm Force is a commercial developer that makes some truly wonderful plug-ins that are unique, sound great, and sport funky interfaces. Their popular freeware filter, Frohmage 1.2, has earned them a following among hobbyists and professionals alike. While the filters that come with GarageBand sound darn good, Frohmage will kick your filter tricks up a notch with its complex set of resonant filter effects, which include distortion and comb filtering alongside the usual cutoff and resonance parameters. And the UI has just as much character as the sound of this wonderful freeware plug.

Figure 8-9
While its user interface may add new dimensions to the word "funky," Frohmage still kicks some serious butt in the filtering department.

After you've tinkered with Frohmage, be sure to check out the demos of their other plugs, like the wonderful Melohman and Predatohm. All of these Ohm Force products are included on the CD-ROM.

Audiofield

If audio mangling tools are more your speed, then Audiofield's Wavebreaker will be right up your alley. While not technically a distortion effect, Wavebreaker is a wave-shaper that outputs a weighted sum of the first ten Chebyshev polynomials. If you want to get into the specifics of the math processing that's involved, you can always Google the term (it's beyond me, and I *love* techno-esoterica). Frankly, with the in-your-face sonic destruction that this plug delivers, *who cares* how they pull it off? Like Expert Sleepers' plug-ins, Wavebreaker is donationware, so if you dig it, tip the developers so they can add even more crunchy algorithms.

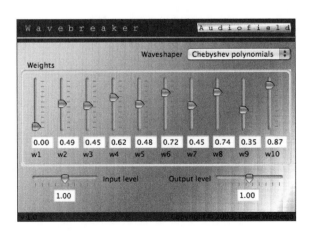

Figure 8-10
What the heck are the "Chebyshev polynomials"? Don't worry, you can skip the math on this one and enjoy the delicious digital distortion effects that Wavebreaker delivers.

Destroy FX

The creators of Destroy FX are part of a collective of programmers called Smart-electronix. While the full catalog of shareware, freeware, and donationware plug-ins created by the Smartelectronix braintrust is too extensive to list here, you can hop on over to www.smartelectronix.com and surf through their plug-in selections. There's some remarkable stuff to be found there, to be candid.

Figure 8-11
When is a reverb *not* a reverb? When it's Destroy FX's remarkable, exotic, and free Transverb plug-in.

One notable plug-in is called DFX Transverb, which in the words of Destroy FX "is like a delay plugin, but it can play back the delay buffer at different speeds. Think of it [as] a tape loop with two independently-moving read heads. There are lots of parameters to control and a parameter randomizer for the impatient."

If you're into really exotic-sounding effects that don't fit tightly into the mainstream production arsenal, the guys at Destroy FX definitely have some goodies for you. Just be sure to turn down your speakers before tinkering—some of their plugs are capable of shredding your speakers if set up incorrectly.

Loop Libraries

Some GarageBand users prefer the convenience and immediacy of pre-rolled Apple Loops. While this standard is still quite new, several forward-thinking developers have hopped on the Apple bandwagon and are providing excellent collections of loops in a wide variety of musical styles. The below list is just a taste of what's out there. Many more loop libraries will surely be released in the coming months, but if you're fiending for more material *right now*, here's where you should begin your quest.

Jam Pack

If it's loops you're after, your first stop should be Apple's first Jam Pack collection. With literally thousands of loops to choose from in a massive range of genres, along with a boatload of new effects and software instrument presets, it's an incredible value for GarageBand users.

The new loops include several hundred drum, percussion, and club-oriented beats, many of which are absolutely current and would work on modern dance-floors with minimal adjustment. Among these beats are nearly a hundred classic drum machine loops with that gnarly '80s vibe. These complement the slew of retro synth loops perfectly, so if electroclash or retronica is your bag, you'll be in heaven. With a touch of hip-hop treatment, they'll also work quite nicely with the smattering of Clavinet loops that are based on the filtered and wah sounds of (get this) '70s cop shows. These loops actually have "cop show" in the loop name—I kid you not! Add one of GarageBand's vibraslaps, and it's *Starsky & Hutch* time!

Continuing with the classic '70s vibe are more than eighty lovely electric piano loops and well over a hundred acoustic piano chord progressions that would sound equally at home in an Elton-inspired pop song or, with a little processing and one of the vibraphone loops, a downtempo trip-hop jam.

Of course, traditional instrument loops are available also, with nearly a hundred real orchestral string, woodwind, and horn passages. These are nicely recorded and work beautifully for cinematic excursions. Rock, jazz, and country are well represented, and quite a few of the guitar loops ably demonstrate the range of guitar sounds GarageBand is capable of when paired with one of the guitar amp-plus-effects presets. There are even a few dobro-esque loops to add some of that down-home flavor to your country/blues jams.

The additional guitar amp and effects presets include everything from '60s surf guitar to that '80s Rockman sound. Cocteau Twins fans will be beside themselves after hearing the lush, chorused effects presets on the "Dreamy Guitar Pattern" loops, which are perfect for spaced-out jams—tailor-made for drifting off or getting romantic. Finally, there's a slew of new sampled instruments that include some lovely sax patches along with a bunch of variations on the factory sounds.

PowerFX

Popular soundware and loop developer PowerFX have ported a sizable portion of their top-notch catalog to Apple Loop format. They've also created a few entirely new products for users of GarageBand (and Apple's Soundtrack) that cover a lot of useful ground.

Dance and electronica producers will want to check out their Electro Clash-matic, Invincible Dance, and Nu Jazz House offerings. Electro Clashmatic delivers modern beats and instrument riffs in classic '80s retro style. Invincible Dance is chockablock full of useful house, techno, and trance selections, while Nu Jazz House caters to those looking for the soulful '70s vibe. Hip-hop fans should definitely peep the Street Stylin collection if they're looking for authentic R&B or old- and new-school beats.

If alt, metal, and classic rock are more your speed, Rock & Pop Trio is a good place to start expanding your loop collection. The aptly named Studio Percussion collection does a nice job of rounding out GarageBand's assortment of beats with some lovely acoustic playing, along with some tasty processed grooves.

All too often, loop manufacturers focus on pure electronica, ignoring other popular genres. If you're a country, Americana, alternative, or even classic '70s AM radio fan, PowerFX's Old + Alt. Country set should get your juices flowing. Connoisseurs of authentic Jamaican sounds should investigate Roots + Raw Reggae's assortment of dubtastic riffs and rhythms.

Those looking for a grab bag of sonic elements in a variety of styles, such as ethnic, dance, urban, and even more mainstream "corporate" stuff, will get some mileage out of the DV Composers ToolKit, whereas iMovie buffs working on their first blockbuster production will delight to the astounding collection of Foley effects and environmental sounds in the Massive FX library.

PowerFX libraries are available directly from www.powerfx.com, as well as their U.S. distributor, Big Fish Audio, www.bigfishaudio.com. It's worth noting that Big Fish is a world-class developer in their own right and will no doubt be developing Apple Loop libraries of their own in the not too distant future.

AMG

Over the years, AMG has released some amazingly popular collections of loops created by big-name artists like Vince Clarke (Depeche Mode, Erasure, Yazoo) and Norman Cook (a.k.a. Fat Boy Slim). These libraries, Vince Clarke: Lucky Bastard and Norman Cook: Skip to My Loops, respectively, have recently been ported to Apple Loop format and work beautifully in GarageBand. The folks at AMG (www.samples4.com) deserve a round of applause for bringing these collections to the GarageBand community, as they're both true classics in every respect.

Other timeless titles in the AMG catalogue include 160dB: The Drum&Bass Interface, Leo Cavallo's 2Step Ahead, Bollywood Dreams, Neil Conti's (of Prefab Sprout fame) Dark Side of the Groove, Ultramagnetic Beats, 9mm Beats, and Urban Search & Rescue—and more are sure to be available by the time you read this.

As this book goes to press, AMG also announced that it is now shipping its newly released ExpansionPack for GarageBand, a collection of 92 sampled instruments for GarageBand including brass, vintage keys (like the Arp Solina and Yamaha CS80), Celtic instruments, mandolin, bagpipes, synthesizers, and more. With an approximate US price of $55, this package looks to be a terrific value.

Bitshift's Bangin' Beats

To celebrate the release of GarageBand, the folks at Bitshift/Glaresoft developed a wonderfully useful 40MB compendium of useful drum loops for electronica, R&B, and hip-hop production called Bitshift's Bangin' Beats. As an added bonus, they've allowed us to include this library on the CD with this book, so be sure to check it out.

Access

In what some have called an astounding display of generosity—and insightful marketing savvy—the synthesizer manufacturer Access has released a sizable collection of free loops created on their top-of-the-line hardware synth, the Virus.

In conjunction with Access, we've included the full library of Access Virus Loops on the CD-ROM. A taste of this virtual analog powerhouse may be exactly the inspiration needed for some users to go out and grab a Virus keyboard of their own. (Since GarageBand can't send MIDI tracks to external synths, the two won't work well together, but you can still record your own Virus loops as audio and then use them in GarageBand songs.) Either way, it's a great-sounding set of hard-edged synth loops for trance and techno. Enjoy!

ReWire

For the uninitiated, ReWire allows two software applications—usually of the sequencing and/or recording variety—to exchange MIDI, tempo, synchronization, and audio information, allowing them to work together as a nearly seamless whole. Remarkably, Apple has integrated ReWire support into GarageBand, making it compatible with the plethora of ReWire applications available, notably Ableton Live and Propellerhead's Reason.

Of course, both of those applications cost several hundred dollars and are considerably more sophisticated than GarageBand. Even so, the inclusion of ReWire has addressed a longtime gripe for some Reason users—the fact that Reason doesn't support track-based audio recording. If you're one of those users, you'll likely be ecstatic to find that you can use GarageBand to record your live instrumentation and vocals, while Reason handles the synthesis and sequencing work.

All you need to do in order to activate ReWire synchronization is launch Garage-Band first, then open Reason. Immediately, Reason will sync with and follow GarageBand as it plays, allowing you to record live overdubs in GarageBand and synth sequences in Reason. Reason's stereo output is blended with GarageBand's main stereo outs, making the entire process completely transparent.

Time-Savers and Helper Apps

Loops, plug-ins, and ReWire aren't the only tools available to extend the usefulness of GarageBand. There are a few shareware widgets out there that offer nifty conversion tools and remote control capabilities via MIDI.

GRBand Assistant

Andy Drabble's GRBand Assistant is a grassroots suite of three software utilities—GB Import, Midi Master, and GB DrumLoops—that enhance GarageBand's ability to work with other data formats, as well as allowing GarageBand to (sort of) import Standard MIDI Files. GB Import is a utility that imports standard .exs sampler files (the format used by Apple's Emagic Logic package) into GarageBand as new software instruments. Midi Master is a utility that uses the sequence information from a Standard MIDI File (SMF) to play music via a sample-based synthesizer. The SMF is rendered to hard disk in AIFF format, and the audio file can then be imported to GarageBand. GB DrumLoops is an application that enables the creation of drum loops in Apple Loop format, which can then be imported into GarageBand or any other Apple Loop–compatible application, such as Soundtrack.

Garage Remote

Murat N. Konar's Garage Remote is a widget that allows any MIDI keyboard that can transmit system-exclusive messages from its buttons to control the transport functions of GarageBand: Play, Stop, Pause, Record, Rewind, and so on.

If you have a compatible MIDI keyboard (Edirol makes several, notably the PCR-50), Garage Remote can definitely reduce the number of trips between MIDI keyboard and mouse, thus streamlining the ergonomics of your compositional process.

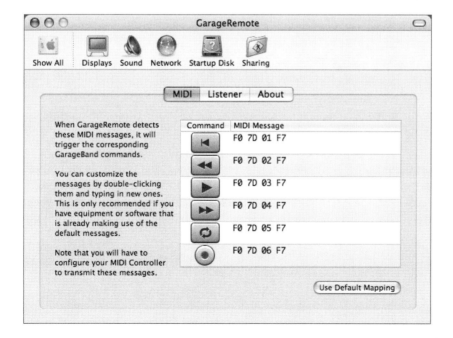

Figure 8-12
If you want to control everything from one spot, Garage Remote may be just the ticket.

Online Resources

Once you've got GarageBand all tricked out with these plug-ins and loops, you'll probably want to share some of your new creations with the world. Fortunately, there are quite a few resources for this. The Internet being what it is, an entire community appeared, literally overnight, after GarageBand was announced.

Figure 8-13
The MacJams web site is chock-full of useful information and news on the latest GarageBand developments.

Your first stops should be www.macjams.com and www.icompositions.com. Both of these sites feature forums, user compositions, tips, and news on the latest developments with GarageBand. Other excellent online resources include www.mac-jukebox.net and www.thegaragedoor.com. Even if you don't post your own work, it's fun to check out what the rest of the world is creating. Some of the compositions are remarkably good, and others, well, I'll leave that for you to discover for yourself.

Acknowledgments

When I told my friends and family that I would be cranking out a complete book on GarageBand in less than three months, there were audible gasps. Generally, writing and researching a technical book of this type takes *considerably* longer. Fortunately for me, I had a lot of support through the process.

I'd like to begin by thanking my fiancé, Seabrook Jones, for putting up with my hectic schedule and helping me juggle life's many responsibilities. I'm truly blessed to have such a generous and supportive partner.

I'd also like to thank my entire family—Papa, Suzi, Som, Karen, Marion, Ami, Niki, Anjuli, and Elly—for encouraging me to pursue my dreams. Many musicians are surrounded by discouragement from family, friends and associates. I'm genuinely grateful that I don't have do deal with that.

Of course, the Backbeat team—Richard Johnston, Jim Aikin, and Amy Miller—all deserve a round of applause for giving me another fabulous book opportunity *and* helping to make me look good in the process.

Christine Wilhelmy and Xander Soren from Apple were a joy to work with. Each took the time to answer my numerous questions and clarify technical details, despite their other professional obligations. Much appreciated!

Last but not least, I'd like to give a shout out to my peeps at Little City, the best little coffeehouse in Texas! These folks turn me on to the latest indie pop, as well as helping me maintain my caffeine buzz as I write. I can't imagine writing a book anywhere else!

On the CD

CD-ROM Contents

All of the software applications on the CD are demos, shareware, donationware, or freeware. The limitations of the demo format vary from product to product: Some quit after a given period of time, some may not include all of the features provided by the full version, and so on. The method by which a fully functioning copy can be purchased also varies, so you'll need to consult the manufacturer's website for details. Direct links to each manufacturer's site are included in their respective folders for your convenience.

The included soundware and samples, which are taken from the developers' catalogs of libraries, are all license- and royalty-free (for music production only) with the exception of the AMG Apple Loops, which are demo only, and thus can't be used in music that you release to the public — see the file titled "AMG_License_ Info.txt" for more information. Also note that PowerFX has generously included a "buy one, get one free" discount with this book, so if you like what you hear, you can go to their website, purchase additional products, and save some bucks.

How to Install Apple Loops in Garageband

Open the GarageBand application and select the Loop Browser window (command+L). Then select the loops you want to add to your collection and drag them onto the file list in the Loop Browser window. You can drag entire folders or just specific files into the window for indexing. If you've dragged complete folders in for indexing, their original names will be retained and they will be placed in the following location: Library/Application Support/ GarageBand/Apple Loops/(folder name). If you've only dragged in specific files, you can find them in Library/Application Support/ GarageBand/AppleLoops/Single Files.

How to install Audio Unit plug-ins

Quit GarageBand, then select the plug-in file (the file with the extension ".component") and move the plug-in to one of the following locations:

Macintosh HD/Library/Audio/Plug-Ins/ Components or ~/Library/Audio/Plug-Ins/ Components/ where ~/ is shorthand for your home directory (/Users/yourname/).

Placing the .component file in the former location will allow all system users to access it, while placing it in the latter location will allow use by only the selected user.

Soundware

Access

Samples and loops derived from their popular Virus line of synthesizers. (Note: The loops are in a Disk Image file [.dmg]. Double-click on the file with the .dmg suffix to mount the file on your desktop, then follow the instructions in the associated install PDF.)

AMG

Demo-only samples and loops from selected libraries. Audio demos of ExpansionPack and SynthPack products.

Bitshift

Custom drum loops.

PowerFX
Samples and loops from selected libraries. License information is contained in the file named "PFX Apple Loops Read me.rtf."

Audio Unit Plug-Ins — Effects

Audiofield
Wavebreaker 1.0 waveshaping effect plug-in. (Note: The plug-in is in a Disk Image file [.dmg]. Double-click on the file with the .dmg suffix to mount the file on your desktop, then move the .component file to Library/Audio/Plug-Ins/Components as described above.)

DestroyFX
Transverb reverb plug-in. (Another .dmg file — see above.)

Expert Sleepers
Multi-tap Delay, PingPong Delay and Phaser plug-ins.

Ohm Force
Freeware Frohmage filter plug-in and demo versions of Mobilohm, OhmBoyz, Predatohm, and Quad Frohmage plug-ins.

Audio Unit Plug-Ins — Instruments

Alphakanal
BuzZer2 software subtractive-analog synth plug-in. (Note: The plug-in is in a Disk Image file [.dmg]. Click on the file with the .dmg suf-fix to mount the file on your desktop, then move the .component file to Library/Audio/Plug-Ins/Components as described above.)

Expert Sleepers
Additive synth and Crossfade Loop Synth instrument plug-ins.

Glaresoft
iDrum 30-day trial demo. (Click on the file with the .dmg suffix to mount the file on your desktop, then double-click on the installer.)

Green Oak
Crystal synthesizer plug-in.

Ohm Force
Demo version of Symptohm synthesizer plug-in.

GarageBand Helper Applications

Andy Drabble
GRBand Assistant demo version. (Click on the file with the .dmg suffix to mount the file on your desktop, then follow the instructions in each of the readme files.)

Murat N Konar
GarageRemote 1.0.1 MIDI-based transport control application.

Index

WHEN IT COMES TO MUSIC, WE WROTE THE BOOK.